BLACK TALK

BLACK TALK

Ben Sidran

New foreword by
Archie Shepp

A DA CAPO PAPERBACK

Library of Congress Cataloging in Publication Data

Sidran, Ben.
  Black talk.

  (A Da Capo paperback)
  Bibliography: p.
  1. Afro-Americans—Music—History and criticism. I. Title.
ML3556.S58 1983   781.7'296073   82-23652
ISBN 0-306-80184-1 (pbk.)

Grateful acknowledgement is made to
Harper & Row, Publishers, Inc., for permission
to quote from Aldous Huxley, *The Doors of Perception*

First paperback printing—March, 1983
Second paperback printing—August, 1986

This Da Capo Press paperback edition of *Black Talk* is an unabridged
republication of the first edition published in New York in 1971, here
supplemented with a new Foreword by Archie Shepp and photo-
graphs by Tom Copi. It is reprinted by arrangement with the author,
who has supplied a new Preface for this edition.

Published by Da Capo Press, Inc.
A Subsidiary of Plenum Publishing Corporation
233 Spring Street, New York, N.Y. 10013

To my father

ACKNOWLEDGMENTS

Steven M. L. Aronson, George Brown, Elliot Eisenberg, Mike Gabriel, Pallo Jordan, Ray Lucas, John Postgate, and Rupert Wilkinson contributed to the conception of this book but are in no way responsible for its shortcomings.

CONTENTS

PREFACE TO
DA CAPO EDITION

The idea of considering Black music in America in light of an oral continuum evolved gradually, after years of listening to the music, after reading McLuhan on Western cultures and speculating on non-Western counterparts, after studying Wittgenstein on semantics and noting the general confusion in the field, and finally after listening to a Coltrane solo and hearing my own mother's voice.

Much of what exists in these pages began as a brief glimpse of a greater truth and ended as a quick sketch of the trail that truth left behind.

The musician *is* the document. He is the information itself. The *impact* of stored information is transmitted not through records or archives, but through the human response to life. And that response is ongoing, in the air, everywhere, an alternative constantly available to those who have ears to hear.

This perspective certainly is not new. To the contrary, it is everywhere. But it wasn't written down, so it wasn't written about.

There is a tremendous irony in trying to re-capture this essence of the oral tradition in a few typewritten pages. And while concepts such as "psychological territory" and "the politics of perception" are considered in the text, it does not seem possible to communicate these nuances to someone not steeped in the music itself.

And there is an additional irony in the fact that, since the initial publication, the thesis of *Black Talk*—"how the music of Black America created a radical alternative to the values of Western literary tradition"—has not been developed by scholars more qualified than myself to examine the larger implications. To this day, the book you are holding remains the only one to consider the music of Black America in this light.

BEN SIDRAN
December 1980
Madison, Wisconsin

FOREWORD

I feel privileged to have been asked by Mr. Sidran to introduce *Black Talk*. First, because I have known the book almost since its initial publication. It has been featured prominently on my book list and I have made numerous references to its concepts in my various lectures and discussions on the subject of African-American music at the University of Massachusetts where I teach.

Let me say, too, that I consider *Black Talk* one of the most important works on the social process by which Black music is communicated—certainly since the appearance of *Blues People* by LeRoi Jones (Baraka). For it illuminates the language of Black music, further clarifying, even updating such earlier classics as *Muntu* and *The Myth of the Negro Past*. It examines and puts to trenchant analysis certain ideas that have heretofore been only hinted at—even by Black authors. Harold Cruse came closest in his work, *Crisis of the Negro Intellectual,* when he made a passionate plea for a dialogue among Black intellectuals for the purpose of establishing a Black "critique" or unified position on art, one that would be politically as well as esthetically cogent.

Sidran, however, goes in another direction. More sociologically oriented, he is able to unearth a different aspect of the truth. For he makes reference to the oral tradition, suggesting its retention in the New World and subsequent transference into a socio-musical entity, with numerous political and symbolic implications. And while this is by no means an attempt on Mr. Sidran's part to give us a complete exegesis of traditional tribal experience, he does offer considerable insight into the functional aspects of the "nommo" factors—if I might inject a Bantu reference.

I spoke with Ben prior to writing this piece and our conversation got me thinking about the oral process and just how it functions among Black musicians. John Coltrane is an excellent case in point. I can remember as a young man in my twenties—with Pharoah Sanders, Rocky Boyd, George Brown (a drummer now living in Europe), saxophonist Marion Brown (no kin to George) and others—requisitioning the great master's time, which he always gave with infinite grace and aplomb. This, of course, would be something less than astounding were it not that Mr. Coltrane's willingness to share his wisdom and profound insights with a younger generation was not exactly the norm among musicians, as is often asserted. In several instances from my own memory I can report that the matter was quite the contrary. Not to say that the oral tradition had stopped working by the time I came along—not by any means. But the old handkerchief over the trumpet keys not only served to confuse wouldbe "white" imitators, but also Black ones. There is a firm belief in this music that (if I may quote Lester Young, second hand) "to join the throng, you've got to make your own song."

Anthropologists and ethnomusicologists use the term "informants" to describe the people who are essential to the transmission of the oral information. The word's unfortunate resemblance to "informers" (which connotes "stool pigeon," someone who is an unwilling—or willing—dupe of another's ploy) is ironic, for this has often been the situation when innocent, untutored people have shared private, esoteric information with self-seeking scholars and recording companies who exploit their subjects for the furtherance of academic research.

Let us consider Mr. Coltrane not as "informant" but as teacher in the highest pedagogic sense, as "guru." In a conversation I had with George Brown a few years ago in Geneva, he reminded me of the reverence and esteem we all had for John and how this came out in our various conversations with him. We were, mind you, not only awed by Coltrane the virtuoso (whose innovations still baffle would-be imitators) but our taciturnity before him was rooted in basic respect, an understanding of the rules regarding "elders." As Brown so poignantly remembered, "We mostly just sat and listened, maybe offering a comment of acknowledgment every now and then. We all recognized our ignorance in the face of his genius."

For a moment I thought back to those early days on Columbus Avenue, where the Coltrane family had moved after coming from Philadelphia. I thought of myself just as George described. This is not to say that we didn't have searching musical questions to ask. But the questions themselves were part of a spiritual matrix in which the personality of the master was more important to the relationship than the rhetorical handling of academic whys and wherefores. It transpired more in the spirit of the training of a Yoruba apprentice carver, than in the creation of a conservatory product.

For example, I remember spending an entire afternoon with John, just listening to him talk about his admiration for Art Tatum, whom he loved (along with Thelonius Monk and Miles Davis) much the same way we loved him. "Art," he said with informed excitement, "would approach a C seventh from the E-flat chord or even as far away as the F-sharp (an interval of an augmented fourth) and resolve it within a space of four beats." (This makes a total of six half-steps, and if we assume that a seventh has a minor counterpart, there are at least twelve possibilities for harmonic improvisation in this simple one-bar contest.)

Mr. Coltrane was then developing his famous "sheets of sound," in which he did on the saxophone the things he heard on Tatum's piano—taking the conception further. I barely understood at that time the implications of this informal conversation. In fact, it took me years to realize the effect of that single afternoon on my overall approach to saxophone playing.

From a performer's standpoint Mr. Coltrane, like his mentor Parker, had an incredible technical ability, the product of prodigious and painstaking practice. Yet his artistry was less a matter of speed or technical prowess than of a certain passion, born of a sense of discipline and integrity almost mystical, yet integral to Black improvised music at its highest level. His virtuosity was rooted in a tradition that had developed long before Joplin composed "The Maple Leaf Rag."

I believe the fundamental source of the characteristic Black musical genius derives from three essential areas of experience: (1) The Afro-Christian Church; (2) the functional song (here defined as the work song, arwhoolie, cries, etc.) as it evolved under slavery; and (3) the various songs, chants; games that come from Black childhood experience.

Prior to World War II most African-American music, though it offered a strong instrumental component, was essentially dance-oriented. And to this extent the prerequisites of "swing" were paramount. Music, as Ellington said, just didn't mean a thing without it—though he himself foreshadowed development of longer, more instrumental forms, even in his early works. But with the coming of the war the cabaret tax on large dance establishments made it prohibitive to hire big bands.

Several conflicting phenomena grew out of this hiatus. As the music gained a wider, more diffuse audience, the community basis was attentuated and the nomenclature was changed. In the twenties all Black music (except ragtime) was termed "race" music to indicate it was the *niggers* who made it. Now with increasing commercial acceptance on records, and later radio, it became rhythm and blues, which somehow encompassed "jazz" as well. This resulted in the division of Black music into arbitrary categories—Blues, Classic Blues, Gospel, Jazz, Ragtime, Soul, Pop, Rock 'n

Roll—without regard to the indivisible nature of its roots. (Why have we never employed terms like impressionistic, baroque, secular, religous, to describe Black music? And if not those terms, since they seem to have been co-opted to define the "Western experience," why not one that gives credit to the true authors of the music, to the theoretical aspects on which it is based?)

Small wonder that, as Neil Leonard points out (in *Jazz and White Americans*), there is a general misconception that Black music is in fact "White American Music"—truly ironic in light of the impressive contribution of the black songsmiths and the oppressive conditions under which they labored, pariahs in the land of their birth. Part of the problem arises from the tags stuck on Black music by some critics —"bop" in the forties and then the "cool school" from the West Coast (depicted by the media as "white" though it was based on the innovations of Lester Young and Miles Davis). Later the Black musicians of the East Coast were pitted as a foil to this cool school, and were themselves dubbed "hard boppers" or the "funk" school. Now I submit—with literary friends like these, does the Black music world need enemies?

But to continue our little historic journey—a metamorphosis occurred when the dancers' images were refocused and dispersed through the plastic medium of sound-imagery. The saxophonist, with his multi-keyed, multi-toned instrument, begat the perfect existential weapon. No one better understood this than Parker, who ultimately unleashed Black music from the prerogatives of dancers. He changed what was essentially a rural music into an urban one. He represented the reintroduction of what Sowande calls the "ritual experience," further identifying this music as diasporic.

The sophistication of this music and its creation in the burning sessions that took place uptown in the forties was a deliberate attempt by the Black composer-performer to form an imagery which, in the words of composer-genius Thelonius Monk, could not be imitated (note: imitation is a primary artistic concept) by the "white boys." Or to put it another way, the *raison d'être* of this new language was the creation of a medium outside the parameters of Western academic theory (musical in this case, though it has other implications).

Ben is deadly accurate here when he says that Black music has transmitted the seeds of Black experience far more effectively than mere words acquired second hand. McLuhan says that "the medium is the message" and Ellington, with his customary eloquence, observed that "all the world is becoming slightly oriental." The process of Black music, and "Black talk" itself, has been the concerted effort by Blacks to discover "roots"—made possible because, as Herskovits states, music constitutes an area of "unconscious focus." Simply listen to an Ellington or Henderson recording from the twenties and see how they capture more than a thousand Gatsbys the *feeling* of the so-called "jazz" era. The Black instrumentalist, apart from the vocalist and dancer, was able to do his own thing in a world where his words were music, and his language was his own.

Read this work and make it a part of your permanent library.

ARCHIE SHEPP
Amherst, Massachusetts
September 1980

INTRODUCTION

This study is both a historical and a thematic approach to the black music of America. I call it a *cultural history* because of its slant: it is not concerned with dates and names so much as with general cultural movements. I have therefore had to exclude several black musicians—many of them are my favorites, and many of them have contributed a great deal to the body of black music—in order to explain the cultural basis for black music in America and examine how black music supports and perpetuates that cultural basis. This study is a radical departure from all other studies on black American music. There are excellent books telling who did what, where and when. There are no books, with the exception of LeRoi Jones's *Blues People,* that look into the cultural *why* of black music. There are no books at all that consider black culture in America as an oral culture and none that treat black music as part and perpetrator of that orality. I should mention here that *oral* and *orality* are never used in their capacity as psychoanalytic terms. The category *oral culture* is used to counter the generic *literate culture,* and not at any time to oppose, for example, an *anal culture.* This study, then, owes much to the pioneering work of Marshall McLuhan, who was among the first to note in writing that the literate base of our society was breaking down—an irony carried to even greater extremes in these pages—and owes very little to the pioneering work of Sigmund Freud.

It should, first of all, be evident that any examination of black culture in America is necessarily an examination of the relationship between black and white Americans. This relationship—the images "black" and "white" that Americans hold of each other—has shaped the cultural evolution of all Americans. Perhaps in the long run, the light shed here on this relationship is more important practically and socially than any one-sided examination of orality could ever be. Let's take the old bromide: "Negroes have a natural sense of rhythm," which has always been considered a "racist stereotype" because it was traditionally used by whites and was based on speculation in genetics for which there was no proof. And yet today, that same bromide, stripped of its genetic implications, has been taken up by militant blacks who seek to turn the fact of their blackness into a club. One articulate young Negro, Julius Lester, has written: "Of the minority groups in this country, blacks are the only one having no language of their own. Language serves to insulate a group and protect it from outsiders. . . . [The Negro] has another language, and that language is rhythm. This has been recognized by black people for some time, and they call it 'soul.' "[1] If white "racists" even at this late date could deliver some genetic evidence for "natural rhythm," nobody, it seems, would be happier than Julius Lester. "Natural rhythm" and genetic evidence aside, how then does one talk about music as the black American's native tongue? One of the central problems of this book has been the difficulty in generating a vocabulary which would be acceptable to all factions and serve the cause of an objective study at the same time that it served to explain the *meaning* of black music as a kind of language.

It was apparent to me from the start that it was possible to combine musical analysis with social analysis. In a sense, the musical group is a prototypical social unit, which evolves prototypical social patterns, rules, relationships, precedents, and *initial thought patterns*. There is, however, an inherent paradox in this study. I agree with Aldous Huxley, who believes that symbol-systems such as formal language are basically formulated to exclude certain kinds of information, to reduce nonrational experience into rational pigeonholes and to verbalize the nonverbal. Semantics, symbolic logic, and psychoanalysis are all means of refining or by-passing speech to get at meaning. But black music is a form of oral communication which itself by-passes formal analysis to communicate some kind of empirical meaning and, beyond that, some form of emotional truth. To write about such a form of communication is often to reduce it to nothing very meaningful.

The subject of my investigation, then, is the social function of black music in America. In these pages, I am mapping the progress of a black, oral culture in America, how it reacted to white America, how white America reacted to it, and the nature of the relationship itself. I try to point out the distinctive elements of black music and relate these to the social process. My basic assumption is that black music is not only conspicuous within, but *crucial to,* black culture. It has often been asserted that music—its place in society and its forms and functions—reflects the general character of the society. It has, however, rarely been suggested that music is potentially a *basis* for social structure. Yet I contend that music is not only a reflection of the values of black culture but, to some extent, the basis upon which it is built. This places on the importance of musical expression a stress alien to the tradition of Western cultures. Music in Western societies is thought of, in general terms, as either popular (low-brow, vulgar) or classical (exalted or art music). The popular music is then dismissed as inconsequential, while the art music is elevated *above* the realm of everyday activity. Western theory tends to detach art from life, just as Western man tends to detach himself from both art *and* life. In black American culture, popular music is the exalted music; it is art that is vulgar in that it is the creation, responsibility, and property of the total community. In this sense, music begins to emerge as a potential foundation for social activity.

In failing to develop a literate tradition, by maintaining instead the subsequent oral tradition, black culture came to rely heavily, if not solely, upon oral modes of communication. These modes necessitate the advanced development of the faculties of vocal expression and aural perception. The development of these techniques accompanies corresponding development in the social system, inasmuch as the social process is a function of the separate psychological orientations of its individual members. Black music can be seen as a function and, to some extent, a cause of a peculiarly black ontology. (I use *ontology* in its dictionary meaning: the science of being or reality, i.e., the branch of knowledge that investigates the nature, essential properties, and relations of being.) Thus, the investigation of black music is also the investigation of the black mind, the black social orientation, and, primarily, the black culture.

The elements of black music make a particularly strong "mood synchronizer": the music can galvanize a group of individuals on an emotional, nonverbal level of experience. This was true centuries ago in Africa—from what little we know of the relationship of music and African religious experience—and it is true today in American ghettos. This significant aspect of black music is often overlooked by the historians—with the result that black music has been a victim of the *selective tradition* of Western literary disciplines. Selective tradition is the survival of a culture through records, "governed, not by the period itself, but by new periods,"[2] and thus creates the historical record of a culture at the same time that it omits considerable areas of what once was a living culture. American literary tradition is concerned primarily with American literary traditions and this, by definition, excludes from examination most of the black experience. The real crisis in American conscience is that there has been no crisis concerning the black culture. Black music, for example, came to light only after it was sold over the counter on an international scale through predominantly white imitations. And even then, only the in-

creasingly tense black "situation" in America focused attention on the source of this music. What this suggests is that
the selective tradition may be breached either by a quantity
which is economically profitable or a quality which is psychologically threatening to that tradition. Black music has both.

Today, America is confronted with a growing black tradition, a very different selectivity generated on both oral and
literate levels by members of the black community to whom
the process itself is not new. There have always been those
black Americans who sought to reject and reinterpret the
traditional view of Afro-American history, notably David
Walker followed by Denmark Vesey, Nat Turner, Frederick
Douglass, and on down through time to Malcolm X. The
only new thing is that today this is happening on a massive
scale with the whole black community participating, to some
extent, in the terminology, technique, and tone of the process.
As black music is—and always has been—the most important single socializing element of black culture, its role in
this process is nothing less than considerable.

Yet black music remains a subject discussed in the streets
more often than in the academies. This is perhaps due to a
more general failure to examine the implications of black
music as they relate to the oral tradition of black culture. I
use the term *oral culture* not simply to establish a random
category to oppose that of *literate culture* because, on the
one hand, all literate cultures grew out of an oral culture
at some point in their evolution: all cultures are more or
less oral cultures inasmuch as communication through speech
and aural perception is common to all cultures. Orality can
be seen as a difference in the degree of stress placed on oral
modes of perception and communication. This leads Western
tradition to view the oral tradition of Afro-Americans as an
inherent lack, a kind of literary vacuum and hinders the
acceptance of orality as a valuable mode of perceptual
orientation. On the other hand, we know that what begins

as a difference in degree can, through centuries of cultural evolution, take on the properties of a difference in *kind*. It can therefore be suggested that orality, besides being a common denominator for all cultures, is, after extended generations, the basis for an alternative breed of culture.

One can easily understand why white, or Western, historians have tended to minimize or omit the study of orality. They are writers by cultural tradition, a tradition which places no value whatever on the absence of literacy, and, as such, they have little if any experience of the advantages of orality. Also, literacy freezes concepts, as it were, through the use of print, making the more fluent oral modes even more elusive. It is remarkable that black authors have failed to investigate this point; it is also very telling, for it suggests that in becoming Westernized, in grasping the advantages of literacy, they simultaneously released their hold on the advantages of orality. What makes this maneuver particularly tricky is that the advantages of orality have rarely been recognized by Western tradition, and black authors are often overly concerned with notions of Western legitimacy. It is also apparent that black authors tend to rush to the defense of black traditions through the idiom of literacy and, in their haste, fail to notice what appears to be the rather insignificant fact of an oral tradition. There have been exceptions—most recently the Dunhill record called *The Last Poets*—but they only serve to prove the rule. The most glaring example of this phenomenon is found in the work of Frantz Fanon, the famous black revolutionary psychiatrist. In Fanon's monumental and now deified work *The Wretched of the Earth,* which Eldridge Cleaver calls the Bible of the black revolution, the chapter on "National Culture" includes a brief two paragraphs on the oral tradition while page after page is devoted to the plastic arts, to painting, to the "African Ballets," and even to black literature.

The question of the relationship of black music to the oral traditions of Afro-American culture, then, is still open inasmuch as the latter has been generally ignored and the former more often exploited than explored. Both the association of music with magic in African cultures and the importance of music to the development of black Christianity in America have been cited as proof of connection between black music and black spirituality. But the crucial point that the foundations of that music and that spirituality stem from an oral tradition and that this implies an inherently non-Western perceptual orientation within the black culture has escaped most Western observers. The end of slavery and the rise of a new black secular tradition in America found the black community creating its own social systems out of the patterns laid down during slavery. The social nature of black music was used to shape both the old and the new social structures. Indeed, future historians may well note that black music was the element that not only provided the basis for a viable social structure during times of crisis for the black community, but was at the heart of the ensuing black social revolution as well.

"In a world where education is predominantly verbal, highly educated people find it all but impossible to pay serious attention to anything but words and notions. There is always money for, there are always doctorates in, the learned foolery of research into what, for scholars, is the all-important problem: who influenced who to say what when? . . . The non-verbal humanities, the arts of being directly aware of the given facts of our existence, are almost completely ignored. . . . Verbalists are suspicious of the non-verbal; rationalists fear the given non-rational facts. . . . Besides, this matter of education in the non-verbal humanities will not fit into any of the established pigeonholes. . . . Systematic reasoning is something we could not, as a species or as individuals, possibly do without. But neither, if we are to remain sane, can we possibly do without direct perception, the more unsystematic the better, of the inner and outer worlds into which we have been born. This given reality is an infinite which passes all understanding and yet admits of being directly and in some sort totally apprehended. It is a transcendence belonging to another order than the human, and yet it may be present to us as a felt immanence, an experienced participation."

—Aldous Huxley
The Doors of Perception

BLACK TALK

1 ✶✷

Oral Culture and Musical Tradition:
Prehistory and Early History (Theory)

It is difficult to say anything definitive about the pre-history of the American Negro. The African cultures from which the slaves were taken kept no written records. The information which did survive in the forms of lore and ritual was generally considered too primitive or too barbaric to be of importance and, subsequently, was not preserved. Yet, the fact that the African cultures had an oral rather than literate base and the instance of cultural isolation within the United States make it possible to suggest a new method for examining the Afro-American experience as a continuum. If the American Negro managed to preserve his oral culture and to extend its base into the greater American society, then there exists in America even today a "subculture" or "counter-culture" with its own social and value structures and a mode of perceptual orientation capable of supporting such structures. The retention of oral culture means the survival of the necessary perceptual attributes. The examination of these attributes, in, for instance, black music, can yield important information about the nature of the oral continuum.

Because of several centuries of commingling with a literate culture in the United States, these oral biases manifest themselves subtly and therefore meet with little resistance from the greater American society. Literate society often turns a deaf ear to the implications of an oral culture. A clue to

1

why this is so may lie in the suggestion that "the function of the brain and nervous system is in the main eliminative and not productive. . . . The function of the brain and nervous system is to protect us from being overwhelmed and confused by this mass of largely useless and irrelevant knowledge, by shutting out most of what we should otherwise perceive or remember at any moment, leaving only that very small and special selection which is likely to be practically useful."[1] Because the literate culture and the oral culture have alternative views as to what constitutes relevant, practically useful information, they impose alternative modes of perception for gathering information. Western culture, it seems, stresses the elimination of perceptual information. The Western view of the witch doctor or schizophrenic as one who receives "too much" of reality indicates this fear of perceptual excess. Although all people have to do certain kinds and amounts of elimination, in oral cultures, members appear to experience a wider range of emotions on a more immediate level of sensation: it appears that the oral man receives more perceptual information as well as perceptual information of a different kind.

Oral cultures use only the spoken word and its oral derivatives, i.e., musical representations of basic vocalizations. This determines the referents of oral perception in general. As Cherry puts it: "The sounds of speech are tied to the time continuum—and the hearer must accept them as they come; time is the current of the vocal stream. But with sight it is different; the eye may scan a scene, or may sweep over the phrases and lines in a book, at varying speeds, as may suit the viewer or reader . . . the stream of words and phrases may be dammed or checked at will. There are then two distinct classes of signal. There are signals in *time*, such as speech or music, and there are signals in *space*, like print, stone inscriptions, punched cards, or pictures."[2] Whereas paper and ink are the medium of the literate man, oral communication is *immediate*. That is, oral communication is free from intervention of a medium. It is a "direct presence." To paraphrase McLuhan, the message is the medium. The oral man thus has a unique approach to the phenomenon of time in general: he is forced to behave in a spontaneous manner, to act and react (instantaneous feedback) simultaneously. As a consequence of this perceptual orientation, oral man is, at all times, emotionally involved in, as opposed to intellectually detached from, his environment through the acts of communication. This can be called the basic *actionality* of the oral personality. McLuhan has characterized this lack of intellectual detachment as contributing to a superior sense of community, a heightened "collective unconscious" and "collective awareness," within oral cultures.[3] It is sufficient for the moment to suggest that sound is fleeting and one must react immediately or lose the perceptual experience entirely.

There are, then, what appear to be two basic *approaches* to perception and the organization of information and, subsequently, two basic approaches toward what constitutes legitimate (i.e., relevant) behavior. These two approaches are alternatives, though not exclusive of each other, and each carries its own advantages. The advantages of the literate orientation are well known through the advance of modern technology and literature. The advantages of the oral mode become manifest in the ability to carry out spontaneous, often improvised acts, of a group nature. These two modes of thought are not a function of different stages of development of the human mind, but are, in Lévi-Strauss's phrase, "two strategic levels at which nature is accessible to scientific enquiry: one roughly adapted to that of perception and the imagination: the other at a remove from it . . . one very close to, and the other at a remove from, sensible intuition."[4] Oral man makes decisions, acts upon them, and communicates the results through an intuitive approach to a phenomenon. The literate man's criteria of what constitute legitimate behavior, perception, and communication often shut out what constitute legitimate stimuli to the oral man. Koestler cites a remarkable experiment which demonstrates that psychological orientation can determine perception at relatively peripheral sensory input levels of the nervous system. This study indicates that the animal blocks off a stimulus from one quarter when a more attractive stimulus appears from another, that the brain's stimulus-seeking activity appears to start in the ear. "In a series of experiments the cat's auditory nerve was tapped and wired to an amplifier, so that impulses (provided by a metronome source) passing from ear to brain were directly recorded . . . the moment a mouse in a glass jar was shown to the cat the firings in the auditory nerve were diminished or ceased altogether: the cat was turning a 'deaf ear' on the metronome. The point of the experiment was to show that the process of stimulus-selection is centrally controlled but sets in at the periphery."[5] Thus, conceivably, literate man can turn a "deaf ear" on stimuli that do not fit into his category of "relevance." (To be fair, it should be noted that "selective attention" works both ways and that it is thus possible that stimuli relevant to the literate man will likewise be tuned out by a member of the oral culture.)

There are many implications here, the most crucial of which indicate that not only is it possible that oral man will be "misunderstood" by the literate man—a failure to communicate—but that literate man will fail to recognize that an attempt at communication is even being made. These oral acts of communication may not be recognized as acts of communication at all and might be totally disregarded. "Attitudes and expectations—the pattern of the behavioral matrix to which the organism is attuned at the time—determine what shall constitute a stimulus and what shall not . . . those aspects of input which are irrelevant will be treated as noise and forgotten 'without leaving a trace.' "[6] Indeed, this utter misunderstanding has been at the heart of the relationship between black and white America and, as will be shown, has contributed to the cohesiveness and coherence of the oral culture.

The basic actionality of oral cultures creates a unique problem of leadership within the oral community. It is difficult to impose organization, in the Western sense, on a group that holds spontaneous improvisation to be the most valuable kind of expression. Recently, this ability of the oral culture to generate its own style of spontaneous leadership, rather than depend on imposed, more formalized leadership, was reported by Stokely Carmichael as his major reason for having left America. "I know I cannot provide the leadership right now in America," he wrote, "[but] that's the beauty of black people—spontaneity will be our saving . . . because that means the CIA cannot pinpoint our leadership and destroy the movement."[7] This is reminiscent of the ghetto humor that surfaced during the Watts "movement": "Chuck [the white man] don't know where it's gonna happen next 'cause we don't know ourselves." It also suggests that attempts to legislate against the activity of the black community or to jail its leadership for "conspiracy" is totally futile. The only way to affect the actionality of the black community is through its source: one must either accept into the mainstream of American life its more legitimate forms of expression or seek means of rechanneling this actionality altogether. The American establishment has failed to grasp this principle, but it has not gone unnoticed by black militants. Huey Newton, National Minister of Defense of the Black Panther Party, was among the first to recognize that "the black community is basically composed of activists. The community learns through activity. The black community is basically not a reading community. Therefore it is very significant that the vanguard group first be activists. Without this knowledge of the black community, one could not gain the fundamental knowledge of the black revolution."[8] As music, in terms of social sanctions, is one of the more legitimate outlets for black actionality—indeed, during various periods of black history, it has been the *only* outlet—it follows that black musicians have traditionally been in "the vanguard group" of black culture. It is not surprising, then, that the Black Panther Party has recently turned to the music industry as an agent in the "revolutionary struggle."[9]

The elements of black music most responsible for the impact it has are the vocalized tone and the peculiarly "black" approach to rhythm. These are essential elements of oral communication in general and allow for communication of a nonverbal nature, often at an unconscious level, to triumph over the rigid classification structure of any linguistic system and to continue in the face of cultural suppression. The vocalized approach is part of the greater oral ability to lend semantic significance to tonal elements of speech. Bornman has suggested that "while the whole European tradition strives for regularity—of pitch, of time, of timbre, and of vibrato—the African tradition strives precisely for the negation of these elements. In language, the African tradition aims at circumlocution rather than at exact definition. The direct statement is considered crude and unimaginative; the veiling of all contents in ever-changing paraphrase is considered the criterion of intelligence and personality. In music, the same tendency toward obliquity and ellipsis is noticeable: no note is attacked straight; the voice or instrument always approaches it from above or below. . . . The timbre is veiled and paraphrased by constantly changing vibrato, tremolo and overtone effects."[10] The semantic value of tonal significance is thus carried over into instrumental playing. The "significant tone" is closely related by Wittgenstein to *meaning* what you say. It cannot be disputed that the oral culture receives information through intonation contouring—from the forms of vocalization as well as the content. The manner in which drums were used to "talk" is typical of this communication mode. The oral man's sensitive ear for timbral subtleties allowed him to use these drums to beat phonetic reproductions of words themselves rather than a primitive Morse code system.[11] It is clear that these tonal elements have survived in modern black speech. Let's take an incident related by a Negro who was recently faced with the practical task of distinguishing the registers of the tonal system of a West African language. He stated that he was "greatly aided in this task by reference to the cadences of Negro speech" he knew from Harlem.[12] And LeRoi Jones's phrase "the irony of Negro speech" certainly points out that these elements still retain their semantic value and aid in circumlocution. The quality of vocalization of tone is a major characteristic of all black communication in America and, particularly, of black music.

The black approach to rhythm, being a function of the greater oral approach to time, is more difficult to define in writing. Capturing the rhythms of African or modern Afro-American music with Western notation is a lot like trying to capture the sea with a fishnet. There have been several good attempts, notably Hodeir's discussion of "swing" in terms of rhythmic tension over stated or implied meter and Blesh's notion of "suspended rhythm," but these were attempts at describing rather than notating this rhythm. It is really not enough to say that rhythmic tension is sustained through the imposition of polyrhythms over a stated or implied meter. The complexity of this rhythmic approach is in large part due to the value placed on spontaneity and the inherently communal nature of oral improvisation. An interesting, if slightly obtuse, example was related by Ralph Ellison who, while in Africa, witnessed a large group of tribesmen dancing to the backfirings of a gasoline engine.

In the oral culture, as derived from the African cultures, there was no distinction made between the "artist" and the "audience." Music, which was an integral part of African religious ritual as well as the daily round and which could last for hours on end until the participants dropped from exhaustion, was created by the group as a whole and allowed for the combination of potentially any number of rhythmic interpretations, any combination of individual personalities. This integration of the individual into the society at such a basic level of experience is the root of black group action-ality. One effect of the oral mode of perception is that in-dividuality, rather than be stifled by group activity or be equated with specialization, actually flourishes in a group context. Thus, members of the oral culture are not differ-entiated by their specialist skills but by their unique emo-tional mixes. "The oral man's inner world is a tangle of com-plex emotions and feelings that the Western practical man has long ago eroded and suppressed within himself in the interest of efficiency and practicality."[13]

The essential nature of communication through rhythm is an unknown quantity due, primarily, to lack of interest on the part of Western science. There have been very general experiments into the effect of music on living organisms,[14] but the specific influence of rhythm has only rarely been in-vestigated. "We are only beginning to investigate this on any scientific basis," admits Williams, "but it seems clear from what we already know that rhythm is a way of trans-mitting a description of experience, in such a way that the experience is re-created in the person receiving it, not merely as an 'abstraction' or an emotion but as a physical effect on the organism—on the blood, on the breathing, on the physi-cal patterns of the brain . . . [a] means of transmitting our experience in so powerful a way that the experience can be literally lived by others . . . it is more than a metaphor; it is a physical experience as real as any other."[15] It is not surprising that the oral culture, being by disposition *physically* involved in communication processes, should rely on rhythmic communication, and it is the inherent nature of rhythm that it should reinforce the quality of group activity in black culture.

Rhythm can create and resolve physical tension. This was suggested in the description of rhythmic tension as the imposition of one time "feel" over the implied or stated "feel" of another meter. Tension is very close in feeling to the perception of pleasure; it is, at best, a positive sensation—at least, a release from boredom. Tension, as created through rhythm, is not just a source of pleasure but is both a catharsis for anxiety and a calming device.[16] Whereas the literate man feels tension in abstractions and builds verbal skyscrapers of inference to court and cultivate tension—thus creating pleasure on a verbal level—the oral man gets his supply of tension through the pulse. Tension released through rhythm is strongly associated with the sexual act. To Western man, Afro-American rhythms have often been particularly associated with this act. The literate man stores information through writing; the oral man stores information through physical assimilation: he *becomes* the information. This process has similarities to physical intercourse on a very general level. The use of rhythm as a cultural catharsis, however, will be seen to have an application more specific to black society.

Another general theory of an oral approach to time can be found in the examination of oral grammars. Rainer Werning, who finds the African time concept as the key to understanding "tribal religious and associated terms," has discovered through the examination of West African grammars that "the African in traditional life is little concerned about the question of time. Time is merely a sequence of events taking place now or in the immediate future. What hasn't taken place or what will probably not occur within

a very short time, belongs to the category of 'non-time.' But
what will definitely happen or what fits into the rhythm of
natural phenomena comes into the category of 'potential
time' . . ."[17] The essential phrase here is "the rhythm of
natural phenomena" which can create a category of "potential time." The perception of this rhythm is partly a function of what has been called the emotional involvement of the
oral culture. Oral physicality, spontaneity, and activation
are all part of this larger coin. The time concept in oral
cultures—as seen in the use of polyrhythms to exploit "potential" time—is a reinforcing agent in the process. Physical
involvement with the rhythms of natural phenomena is the
"message of oral communication." Thus all oral communication is a *direct* reflection of the immediate environment and
of the way in which members of the oral community relate
that environment. Rhythm can also be used to manipulate
the greater environment, inasmuch as alterations in time
concept can affect the general "structure of feeling" of the
culture as a whole.[18]

McLuhan has suggested that "great cultural changes
occurred in the West when it was found possible to fix time
as something that happens between two fixed points. From
this application of visual, abstract, and uniform units came
out Western feeling for time as duration . . . our sense of
duration and impatience when we cannot endure the delay
between events. Such a sense of impatience, or of time as
duration, is unknown among nonliterate cultures. . . . For
the clock to dominate, there has to be the prior acceptance
of the visual stress that is inseparable from phonetic literacy."[19] Mellers has gone even further in suggesting that
"Time is only a European notion." He continues, "The
rhythm of the human body and senses, precisely because it
is human, will always be slightly different from, although
related to, the metrical beat of Time; and Spengler may
have been more than merely ingenious in identifying the

post-Christian obsession with Time, as metrically exemplified in European music, with the Decline of the West."[20] Wild though these claims may be—for who can guess what the attitudes of ancient civilizations were?—they do have their application to Afro-American music. Time in the Western sense is a translation from motion-through-space. Time in the oral sense is a purer involvement with natural occurrences and perceptual phenomena. The development of rhythmic freedom has generally preceded social freedom for black Americans. Thus, the time concept, as translated through musical rhythms, has affected the social situation of the oral culture. Rhythm provides an outlet for black aggression and, as such, is the "cultural catharsis" Fanon has suggested is necessary to black culture; rhythm is the expression of the black "cultural ego," inasmuch as it simultaneously asserts and preserves the oral ontology. The initial rhythmic freedom of black music was immediately restricted upon the institution of slavery. Its gradual return to black music was nothing less than the reemergence of the black ego, which had, only after the fact of music, been able to exert itself in political spheres. It is on this basis that black music can be seen, once again, as a source for black social organization: an idea must first be communicated before it can be acted upon. In the case of black music, the idea and the act are one: "The process of communication is in fact the process of community."[21]

That the oral approach to time has surived in America is attested to in a recent report issued by the Center for Applied Linguistics, which states that "Black English" should be treated as a separate form of the English language since "there is no time element in Black English. There is a concept of time, but the language itself is not time-oriented. Black English is not a chronological documentation of life, as is standard English. It is an extension of the whole way of life of black people."[22] The similarity between this assessment and Werning's remarks on the African time concept is striking. The survival of this time conception is both a cause and an effect of the oral approach to rhythm: there is, finally, what appears to be a cyclical relationship between the *concept* of time and its perpetuation through the *application* of rhythm, rather like the relationship between the chicken and the egg.

The oral culture survived in the New World and was retransmitted and reinforced in America through speech patterns (the grammars) and through musical idioms. The slave was taught what little English he was required to know, gathered what else he could, but was rarely, if ever, exposed to formal education. "This being the case," writes Turner, "and since grammar and idiom are the last aspects of a new language to be learned, the Negroes who reached the New World acquired as much vocabulary of their masters as they initially needed, pronounced these words as best they were able, but organized them into their aboriginal speech patterns . . . their peculiarities being due to the fact that they comprise European words cast into an African grammatical mold."[23] This phenomenon has often been reduced to the impression that slaves simply spoke a bad version of standard English. However, one of the theorems of semantics is that the essence of language is partially expressed through grammar, the corollary being that the use of a word is its meaning in a language.[24] Retaining the original grammatical form of speech was tantamount to recomposing America in terms of Africa, as the instance of "Black English" attests.

It also appeared at first that the slaves were unable to master the simple diatonic scale of Western music, inasmuch as their songs all had "blue notes," or areas in the scale where tones were smeared together through melisma. (See Bornman's remarks on "circumlocution.") Indeed, it was the semantic value of intonation contouring that was the source of this melisma. The slaves introduced cries and moans into simple Western songs, giving the white society the impression that they were both children and born entertainers, as both these categories relate to "overemotionalism." The "blue" areas—traditionally the flat third and flat seventh steps, later the flat fifth step of the key—as well as the cries and shouts were instances of intonation carrying a nonverbal kind of information, an application of the diatonic scale unexploited outside oral cultures. It should be noted that this galvanization of meaning and pitch into a single vocalization is found in many oral cultures. The African and Afro-American cultures, however, used these particular "blue" areas of tonality. One psychologist, Dr. Milton Metfessel, has attempted to chart and analyze black American singing and has suggested that there is, in fact, a strong connection between African vowel pitch and black vocalization.[25]

The message carried by this vocalized approach was perhaps initially one of resignation. Although there must have been a longing for escape and freedom, as well as resistance and revenge in the background, the slave initially showed his antipathy to America through apathy. Jones has suggested that the nature of the lyrics to work songs was "underground" material, that seemingly innocent words had multiple meanings, and that therefore the music was more than it seemed. Yet this "underground" sentiment during the nineteenth century was perhaps best likened to the secret language of schoolchildren: the call of today's revolt was there, but it was certainly qualitatively different. I suggest that the vocalized tone was as important to the black revolution as were the double entendres. This communication through intonation operated at an emotional level, more basic than that of verbal interchange. The use of the cries and melismatic approach was also a means of bringing out the individualism in an otherwise destroyed personality; the slaves were only able to express themselves fully as individuals through the act of music. Thus each man developed his own "cry" and his own "personal sound."

The development of "cries" was thus more than a stylization; it became the basis on which a group of individuals could join together, commit a social act, and remain individuals throughout, and this in the face of overt suppression. It has been suggested that the social act of music was at all times more than it seemed within the black culture. Further, to the extent the black man was involved with black music, he was involved in the black revolution. Black music was in itself revolutionary, if only because it maintained a non-Western orientation in the realms of perception and communication. Whereas Western communication theory is based on the notion that "speech contains much that is redundant to intelligence and therefore wasteful of bandwidth,"[26] making it possible for cybernetics to reduce communication to digital, yes/no systems,[27] black communication maintains the integrity of the individual and his "personal" voice in the context of group activity. Thus, the notion that voice tones are superfluous to communication is absurd within the framework of the oral culture. This truth can be applied to instrumental music as well. Whereas Western musicians are recognized for their ability to conform to and master traditional techniques, black musicians are highly regarded for their ability to invent personal techniques and to project personal sounds, the personal techniques being the means whereby the personal sounds are accomplished. As John Coltrane has said, "I recognize an individual when I see his contribution; and when I know a man's sound, well, to me that's him, that's the man. That's the way I look at it. Labels I don't bother with."[28]

Du Bois reported that "one ever feels his twoness—an American, a Negro; two souls, two thoughts, two unreconciled strivings. . . . From the double life every American Negro must live, as a Negro and as an American . . . from this must arise a painful self-consciousness, an almost morbid sense of personality."[29] Traditionally, this dubiety within the black personality has been attributed to external sources, i.e., the white man's rancor and his arbitrary power. The black psychologists Grier and Cobbs have developed around this thesis the notion of the "Black Norm": they pose the concept of a potentially "healthy" kind of cultural paranoia growing out of the climate of overt racism.[30] And yet, although the black culture is quite possibly schizophrenic— living one life for the benefit of white society, another life for itself—I feel it would be faulty to attribute this wholly to the white man's malice, and faultier still to think of the "Black Norm" as a completely negative aspect in the evolution of the American Negro. I would suggest, for example, that the inherently "underground" nature of the oral orientation in the context of literate society has accelerated the dubiety of the black experience and that the subsequent challenge posed to Western value structures which arose through this dubiety was ultimately a constructive element for all Americans. As Jones has said, "The Negro could not ever become white and that was his strength; at some point, always, he could not participate in the dominant tenor of the white man's culture."[31] This strength has been shared by all Americans, black or white, who at any point took exception to the underlying assumptions of mainstream society and has been available simply through the experience of black music.

The "underground," or "counter-cultural," nature of black music in America first surfaced in the work songs of the slaves. These songs were encouraged by the white man because they helped the slaves work more efficiently. But the fact that these songs did accompany work drastically restricted their influence, because the hands and feet could not be used to promote group coherence through rhythms. The work songs did provide a kind of cohesion, though, in an otherwise decimated society in that they provided some outlet for group activity which was not wholly controlled by the white man's influence. The revolutionary aspects of vocalization, which were expressed by a leader and encouraged by the response of a chorus—the basic antiphonal pattern of almost all Afro-American music—were central to these songs. Group improvisation was restricted to this call/response pattern and to the improvised lyrics. Most importantly, the work songs constituted a social act, committed en masse by the black culture, during a period when mass activity was outlawed. It was not until the rise of a black Christian tradition that the music of the oral culture began to reassert itself. The rise of the Negro spiritual can be seen as the first step taken by Negroes to turn their backs on Africa, or to embrace a peculiarly *American* heritage, while at the same time it was a sign of the reemergence of their oral tradition, since that tradition and musical freedom are one and the same. The lack of rhythmic freedom in the work songs was matched by a lack of social freedom, and it is interesting to note that both freedoms, rhythmic and social, developed simultaneously several generations after the work songs.

Although the great hollow-log drums were outlawed because they could be used to communicate literal messages of rebellion, the black culture still managed to reintroduce rhythmic freedom through the use of foot stamping, hand clapping, and small rhythm instruments. Because the slaves had a cultural precedent for the adoption of new gods within the original African religious format and since the second and third generation slaves were becoming Americanized, conversion to Christianity was readily improvised, years before it became acceptable to white society with Quaker missionaries taking an active interest in the souls of the slaves during the nineteenth century. The earliest black "Christian" rituals were clandestine meetings, without the sanction of white society, and were based, in form, on the white "camp meetings" of the period. Baptism was particularly attractive to the slaves when Christian practices became less covert because it included certain water rituals that happened to resemble those of the African river gods, the strongest in the African hierarchy. Most importantly, "spirit possession" was renovated from its African form. This use of music to create a fusion of spirit and flesh is perhaps more important than the fact of the survival of overt Africanisms. This aspect of black music has survived long after the resecularization of black culture: black music became, ultimately, a kind of popular religion in and of itself, retaining the important socioreligious properties that had been developed during the earliest neo-Christian rituals.

Music, then, was not only something to do but also a *way* of doing it. For the black culture, particularly during times of great cultural suppression, it was an act of physical, emotional, and social commitment. Black music was thus not escapist in nature, as was most popular culture during the past two centuries, but was a direct reflection of the combined experiences of many individuals, all of them grounded in reality.[32] The communal nature of black music never lost its impact, as the integration of the individual into the society is one of the primary functions of oral modes. In the Christian rituals, for example, all members were deeply involved, there was no "audience" and no "artist." "The attitude of the spectators was of concerned interest," reported Herskovitz, "the sanctimonious behavior that is associated with European religious exercise was quite absent."[33] There remains to this day no real separation between life and art in black music. Although black musicians have been recognized as "artists" because of their superb mastery of Western instruments, Western song forms, and Western harmonic structure, their music is a direct reflection, as well as an indirect cause, of social activity within the black community.

As Charles Parker, often cited as the greatest black artist of this century, has said, "Music is your own experience, your thoughts, your wisdom. If you don't live it, it won't come out of your horn."[34] The spontaneous nature of black culture keeps this music alive, and the life of this music prevents black culture from dying the death of assimilated Western subcultures.

The way in which the oral culture has survived in America defies category because it rests on the ability to transcend categorization. This ability is a function of the larger oral outlook toward time and the subsequent emotional involvement with events *as they happen*. Literate men are prone to use words which force them into simple opposites. This is especially true of written words that depend on the logic of contrasts, types, and polarities for their meaning. The failure to categorize emotional content along the rigid lines of verbal definition, a result of the stress on vocalization, has thus aided the survival of the black culture; the celebration of the feeling of any given moment as a unique experience, rather than as a part of some elaborate syntactical structure, has made the black man flexible and helped him to improvise. A black love song, for example, is not *just* a black love song—for instance, these lyrics: "I can't stand you, Baby, but I need you—you're bad, but you're oh so good." This is not just word play or semantic juggling, but a sign of the spirit of black culture. One blues singer even recorded the lyrics "I love the blues, they hurt so nice." The oral culture is primarily a living, organic organization, rather than a technocratic structure, and it rails against compartmentalization. Black music communicates on a broad level of experience, often thriving on what should appear to the analytic mind as emotional paradoxes. One black musician, for example, described his music as "playing love and get-out-of-town at the same time." Another black musician said, "I think black people in America have a superior sense when it comes to expressing their own convictions through music. Most whites tend to think it's below their dignity to just show suffering and just show any other meaning that has to do with feeling and not with technique or analysis or whatever you call it. And this to me is why the black man has developed in the field of music that the white man calls jazz."[35] The ability to experience and communicate emotional content on such a broad level is characteristic of the oral man's failure to "detach" intellectually—to not categorize, specialize, or analyze—and is, ultimately, a strong point in the survival of the Afro-American culture. The oral tradition is, even more than a way of experiencing, a manner of presentation. This accounts, in part, for the *universality* of black music, for the acceptance of this music by peoples of all cultures and, especially, by people who are in some way oppressed.

The institution of slavery precipitated the rise of Christianity in black music and society for two major reasons. First, because the slave was absolutely dependent on the white man, he was psychologically impelled to absorb as much of the white culture as he could. He was forced, as Elkins pointed out, to see the white authority figure as somehow really "good."[36] This meant, in effect, seeing the white man's God as somehow good. Second, the black culture, being an oral culture, required an outlet for emotional expression, and all secular outlets had been blocked or denied. The Preacher took the role of lead singer, the group actionality was generated by the vocal and rhythmic response of the congregation (they were all lead singers, group singers, and rhythm players), and the musical-religious ritual became the most important single experience in the daily life of the slave, much as it had been in preslavery Africa. From the beginning, black Christianity was potentially a non-Western, if not anti-Western, institution. Jones writes that "the autonomy of the Christian Negro religious meetings made it the only area in the slave's life where he was free to express himself as emotionally as possible."[37] Further, the development of a musical tradition, as opposed to a literate tradition, or, indeed, even a tradition in any of the visual arts, indicated the basic, cultural inclination of black America. This can be seen as part of the more general "tendency of groups to adjust toward that class of communication patterns which will permit the easiest and most satisfying flow of ideas."[38] Music was as important to the culture as was the church doctrine, the latter gaining currency, in part, because of its resemblance to African religious practices. Indeed, the way Christian ideas and rituals were adopted reflects both this African precedent and the important role of music. "Spirit possession" became the manifestation of the Holy Ghost and was always generated through music. It was felt that "the Spirit will not descend without song." Dancing in church was shunned by Western custom, but the slaves defined dancing as "crossing the feet" and developed "shuffles" and "ring shouts" where the legs were never actually crossed, and the dancers gained great momentum, moving to the rhythm of foot stamps, hand claps, and vocal encouragement. The physicality of this exercise typifies the marriage of Spirit and flesh through black music. Black Christianity existed by virtue of the facts of both black music and black orality; it was probably not the doctrine that was attractive to the black culture so much as the opportunities for improvisation Christianity provided.

Christianity also provided black culture with personality archetypes, and these too involved the status of music and the musician. The close relationship of tension released through rhythm and pleasure perception made black religious ritual an enjoyable experience that easily came to be valued over the more abstract doctrines. The role of the black Preacher became that of performer as well as that of black truth-teller. Given the slave's condition of irrational bondage, it is not surprising that the Christian notion of inherent, or original, sin did not find a fertile climate in the black conscience in which to take root. Worship was more pleasure than exorcism of guilt, more release of emotional energy than lesson-learning. The Devil came to represent to the black culture not the perpetrator of original sin but a hero in evil, a Good/Bad figure, in keeping with the oral ability to transcend categorical polarizations. Indeed, the Devil, according to Grier and Cobbs, was later found in the romantic image of the "bad nigger," the free and independent black man who brought fear to the white culture through threat of physical and/or psychological violence, and "devil music" was associated with good-time music that existed outside the church. Herskovitz has characterized this oral religious outlook as the "deification of accident" and the phrase is particularly apt in relation to black Christianity. The Devil was a "trickster," some say based on Legba, a West African god, who imposed external misfortune on the black man— hence the notion of "deification of accident" or the exaltation of fortuitous events. Thus, the black condition could be viewed by the black man with an eye toward Ultimate Justice, for Fate had proved more reliable, and more accessible, than any of the teachings of Christianity. "Crossing the River Jordan," a concept as well as a song title from the Moody and Sanky hymnal, depicted deliverance in the afterlife as well as in the here-and-now, both of which appeared equally improbable to the slave.

Yet the overwhelming importance of the church structure to the lives of the slaves was menaced from within as well as from without. On the one hand, as the church became more established, it began to shape itself more fully in the image of white institutions and white value structures. The church began to provide social stations among Negroes that were based, ultimately, on the acceptance of these white values:

the Negroes who most resembled whites, either in behavior, dress, or skin pigmentation, assumed the highest status in the church; those with the darkest skin color or with "heathen ways" (meaning, in substance, acting like a black rather than a white man) were ostracized outright. While this system was attractive to blacks who aspired to middle-American values, the incompatibility of "white ways" and "black ways" came to a head within the black lower class. After several generations of slavery, it was not uncommon for the more proper blacks to consider their unassimilated brothers as actually subhuman; black slaveowners were not completely unknown or unheard of. This attitude was enhanced by the caste distinctions of the late nineteenth century between pure Negroes and Creoles, mulattos, and others who regarded themselves as superior. The church was able to gain for its regular members certain advantages, mostly financial and therefore, in time, social and began a vested interest in white society that ultimately led to its acceptance of the separate-but-equal philosophy so perplexing to Du Bois and others. Thus the church, once the bastion for blacks seeking freedom of expression and escape from the white man's control, became the stronghold of the very mentality it was established to circumvent. And in focusing too strongly on the notion of life-after-death, the church little by little became the purveyor of do-nothing conservatism in this life.

On the other hand, the instance of Emancipation radically altered the rules of the game all Negroes, particularly lower-class Negroes, were forced to play. Inasmuch as it was only as slaves that Negroes had had a *place* in American society, those blacks who did not gravitate toward the social structure of the church after Emancipation were alienated from white society even more thoroughly than they had been during slavery. The legislation and enforcement of social and economic segregation—the application of the Puri-

tan "work ethic" in a biased job market—further separated the black, oral tradition from that of the dominant,
literate culture. However, regardless of whether the lower-
class Negro accepted or rejected the values of white society
through his relationship with the black church, he was reaffirming his own oral tradition through the art of music. The
importance of this phenomenon was long overlooked, primarily because music has no artifact. The effects of an oral
tradition do not exist at the levels of material objects or
rationalized opinions but, rather, affect perceptual orientation and thus alter socialization steadily and with little resistance. When the black church instigated the split between
middle-class and poor blacks—thus accepting the "economic
sensibility" of the white culture, Brooks Adams's term
signifying the "triumph of the economic mind over the
imaginative"—the majority of the black population had only
the oral tradition for support and guidance. This meant the
reliance on music sans Christianity or Christian doctrine
and, hence, the emergence of a secularized, professional
musician.

As implied, the rise of music as a *profession* in black
America, not reaching fruition until the migration of large
numbers of Negroes to urban ghettos, parallels the fall of
black Christian authority and the upswing of legal disen-
franchisement of blacks following Reconstruction. This
would date the origin of the secular, professional black musician at some time during the last few decades of the nineteenth century. Although the church remained important
to the black community, it was not nearly the unifying
element it was during slavery. With the legal end of slavery,
Negroes did not need the church as a sanctuary; more and
more "devil music" was played. However, it took many
years to develop a secular music tradition that approached
the rhythmic freedom—and thus the group actionality and
coherence of expression—found within black churches. This

suggests that although the black man was not free within the confines of church authority, it took many years for him to be able to replace the church structure with something equally autonomous and unifying. Black musical idioms reflected this heightened alienation and, later, came to replace the abandoned church structure. Outside the church, music was either produced by the solo black musician—a concept not known before in the oral tradition, as it would have been seen to reflect the alienation of the individual from the organized community—or by the black circus or marching bands, a kind of assimilation of white forms. There was not a substantial black secular music, in fact, until urbanization provided economic markets that could support a professional black musician.

Following Emancipation, freedom was equated with mobility, and thousands of questing Negroes took to the roads (establishing a pattern which was to become part of the black self-image in America). The traveling musician, who had taken on the role of truth-teller from the black Preacher, the role of trickster, or "bad nigger," from the Devil, became the ultimate symbol of freedom. Escape from the monotony and static hopelessness of black employment, combined with the potential for earning a living without having to rely on the white man—beating the white man at his own game, in other words—kept the musician's status high. (In fact, only those musicians who didn't mind traveling became famous; hence mobility had a direct bearing on the black musician's status. This is true even today.) Ultimately, however, the survival of the black musical tradition and, hence, the black oral tradition depended on the ability of the Negro in the North, earning five dollars a day in Henry Ford's factory, to support both local and traveling musicians. This principle—that black culture and black economics support each other and that left to the whims of white society neither would probably exist—remains as true today as at the turn of the century, as can be seen in President Nixon's currently faltering "Minority Capitalism" program.

The peculiarly American character of the Negro was manifested in the combination of the soloist (the Western influence) and the vocalized tone of the music. McLuhan has written that "with the first printing of musical scores in the sixteenth century, words and music drifted apart. The separate virtuosity of voice and instruments became the basis of the great musical developments."[39] Black music established a different trend by including vocal technique as part of instrumental technique. The first black solo musician on the scene was the blues singer, who generally accompanied himself on the guitar, using a loose and open progression of Western chords and a highly vocalized tone with his instrument. The guitar tended to support and imitate the voice. These musicians composed their own songs, based, for the first time, on the secular problems of the black individual. Jones writes, ". . . this intensely personal nature of blues singing is also the result of what can be called the Negro's 'American experience.' African songs dealt, as did the songs of a great many preliterate or classical civilizations, with the exploits of the social unit . . . the insistence of blues verse on the life of the individual and his individual trials and successes on the earth is a manifestation of the whole Western concept of man's life . . . the weight of just what social circumstances and accident came together to produce the America that the Negro was a part of, had to make itself part of his life as well."[40] Yet, although "the whole concept of the *solo*" was relatively unknown in West African music, there is an essential point to add to Jones's observation: the black culture assimilated white culture by accepting its forms while drastically altering its content. The new black individualism, spun-off from the church split and exemplified by the soloist, was unlike traditional Western individualism in that it did not proceed down the chain of inference established through Hobbes, Locke, and Rousseau.[41] Oral cultures do not begin from the assumption of the separation of man from man, nor of man from the environment at large; black individualism has an African heritage in which the individual and his rights are not separated from society. Also, black individuality comes out of action and feeling, as opposed to the *abstraction* of "rights" communicated through literature. It therefore becomes possible to consider *psychological territory*, invisible to the eye but defended as tenaciously as physical territory, as a factor in the peculiarly American character of the black oral tradition.

The Negroes who found that earning five dollars a day in the factories of the North was an improvement over earning nothing in the fields of the South also discovered that they were unprepared to accept certain psychological postures of the urban middle and working classes. In addition to their natural distrust of whites and their growing distrust of the black middle-class institutions, the urban Negro masses were thoroughly alienated from Western values by an almost intuitive mechanism. The Negro, unlike all other ethnic groups in America, has never been assimilated into the greater society, not simply because he was not allowed to nor because he did not choose to, but because in time it became psychologically impossible for him to be. The climate of racism in America has always been clouded by such factors as the translation of *psychological* territory into *physical* actuality. Mailer suggests that "any race problem is anathema to power groups in the technological society, because the subject of race is irrational. At the very least, race problems seem to have the property of repelling reason."[42] Mailer is right to see the failure of blacks to become assimilated into the mainstream of American life as a natural consequence of the incompatibility of alternative psychological postures: "A technological society can deal comfortably with people who are mature, integrated, goal-oriented . . . white or white-oriented. The technological society is not able to deal with the self-image of separate peoples and races if the development of their self-image produces personalities of an explosive individuality. We do not substitute sticks of dynamite for the teeth of a gear and assume we still have an automatic transmission."[43]

With the introduction of the blues to the urban population of the North, there was a confrontation between the warring white and black factions of the Negro personality. In the early part of the twentieth century, Negro musicians in Harlem who were particularly concerned with white notions of legitimacy had taken to playing a written form of music known as "ragtime." This was basically a perversion of commercial and white-oriented music, embellished with various harmonic flourishes. The approach was relatively intellectual and technical, in the Western meanings of these terms, and attested to the urban Negro's desire to master white values and be accepted by white authority structures (i.e., to be "legitimate") seen to be superior. ("If you're white, you're right, if you're black, get back.") It was basically a piano music, conforming to the nonvocal properties of the instrument and lacked the great rhythmic drive that generally characterizes black music. The watered-down rhythmic aspect of it was perhaps the core of its appeal to whites. Much like the Harlem "Literary Renaissance" of the 1920s, ragtime was an attempt by the black man to step up and take the *theoretical* place he was *theoretically* being offered by white society. Ragtime was a composed rather than an improvised music, and, although the best of the composers such as Scott Joplin occasionally gained recognition, was short-lived within the black community. During the tenure of ragtime, Southern musicians brought their more emotional music—the blues—to the city, and although these musicians were themselves considered "country," i.e., backward and socially inferior, their *approach* to music was quickly taken up by the majority of black musicians. The implications of this shift in allegiance were socioeconomic as well as emotional, as they involved all facets of the Negro's self-image. The direction of the cultural flow was clearly marked: "There wasn't an Eastern performer who could really play the blues. We later absorbed how from the Southern musicians we heard, but it wasn't original with us," said the Negro musician Garvin Bushell. "Most of the Negro population in New York then had either been born there or had been in the city so long they were fully acclimated. They were trying to forget the traditions of the South; they were trying to emulate the whites."[44] The Northern Negroes "didn't put that quarter-tone pitch" into the music as did Southern Negroes. In the North they played "a lot of notes"; in the South, they used the quarter-tone pitch because it was the basis for the "cry"—the vocalization—of instrumental playing. The reference that Bushell made to "a lot of notes" implies the Harlem Negro's acceptance of the white sensibility: calculated techniques and arithmetic content were reflected in the feeling of the music.

The *timing* of a period of history—that sense of pace, or urgency that was the heartbeat of the dominant social organisms—is sometimes reflected most clearly in the music of the period. This is especially true in America, for, on the one hand, America has had a strong oral, or story-telling tradition and has always had to struggle to develop a literate one. On the other hand, black music developed in America rather than in European countries, and this music is built on the expression of contemporary emotions. Black music is the "art form" closest to life forms; indeed, its execution depends on mastering certain breathing techniques, its rhythm is "alive" and its instrumental technique is closely related to speech and hearing. The rise of the recording industry is one of the most significant aspects of the twentieth century if only because it facilitated the preservation of this "life." The recording industry gave the product of the oral, immediate culture a kind of permanence; thus, recording is the only true artifact of the oral culture. This industry did not appear, however, until after the effective demise of the ragtime idiom, and thus the real effects of the injection of blues into New York cannot be measured as easily as can labor statistics or suicide rates for the period. But, if seen as a small moment in the long process of black culture seeking its own level within the United States, it becomes one more watermark with which to gauge the black man's progress. A new style of playing evolved after the blues arrived in the North that shifted the focus away from the piano toward the more "vocal" instruments such as the trumpet and, later, the saxophone. The written music, ragtime—although it did survive in vestigial form well into the "swing era" (i.e., Benny Goodman's "King Porter Stomp")—fell by the wayside after the injection of the nonwritten, vocal blues. When the written, or composed, form of jazz resurfaced in the arrangements of Don Redman and Fletcher Henderson, it owed much in both style and content to the blues idiom. Even a new "pianistic" tradition, that of the "barrelhouse" piano players, became prevalent, incorporating a vocal approach to the instrument with a newfound rhythmic drive (much like the Chicago boogie-woogie pianists of the thirties). Barrelhouse piano was not evolved from ragtime piano—the two were, in fact, contemporary idioms: barrelhouse piano came out of the brothels, ragtime piano out of the "polite" world—but was part of the greater process of selection going on within the black culture. The *psychological territory* of the oral culture was being defended.

2

The Black Musician in Two Americas:
Early History—1917

The idea of two separate Americas, one white and one black, was articulated in the "separate but equal" doctrine. One year after Booker T. Washington's "Atlanta Compromise" speech of 1895 in which he put forward this doctrine, the idea became a reality when the Supreme Court upheld Jim Crow laws in the *Plessy v. Ferguson* case. The insights of black men since that time, particularly Du Bois and Garvey, have helped further articulate the separation and so, ironically, have given meaning to a basically irrational law. By the late sixties, the black culture's definition of this separateness had reached startling proportions, with the more militant blacks demanding land from the government and money from the church or seeing the reality of separation in international terms: "We're colonial subjects in a decentralized colony," wrote Cleaver, "dispersed throughout the white mother country in enclaves called black communities, black ghettos."[1] Perhaps the most important single characteristic of legal segregation was the irrational, or at "best" illogical, racial prejudice upon which it was based; irrational inasmuch as the myths condemning the Negro to the lowest rung on the evolutionary ladder had become law, yet they no longer had the ideological frame-

30

work of slavery for support. The "Black Codes" and "peon-age laws" that sprang up in the South created the *actual* separation between black and white America. The nature of these codes was clearly recognized by one Negro attempting to claim his duly elected seat in the Georgia House of Repre-sentatives: "Never in the history of the world has a man been arraigned before a body clothed with legislative, ju-dicial or executive functions, charged with the offense of being a darker hue than his fellow-men . . . never before has a man been arraigned, charged with an offense committed by the God of Heaven Himself."[2] But while the black man during the nineteenth century knew he was not free, he nonetheless expected to be free in the near future. The whole basis for the "Atlanta Compromise" was Washington's theory that "progress in the enjoyment of all privileges that will come to us must be the result of severe and constant struggle rather than of artificial forcing. No race that has anything to contribute to the markets of the world is long in any degree ostracized."[3] From Emancipation until very recently, the American Negro has attempted to defeat the blatant and growing irrationality of his suppression by proving himself *worthy* of freedom, not only a thankless task but one which was quite contrary to the basic assumptions of American society. And, ironically, when the American Negro did enter the markets of the world, the product he had to offer, and that which was accepted wholeheartedly by peoples of all cultures, was the product of his ostracism: his music.

Black culture in America has been shaped by the amount of the psychic energy it has spent adjusting to white culture. In the process, it has come into conflict with the Anglo-con-formity of American life, or the "desirability of maintaining English institutions (as modified by the American Revolu-tion), the English language, and English-oriented culture patterns as dominant and standard in American life."[4] The conflict exists on many levels and manifests itself in both the acceptance and the rejection of Anglo-conformity. In either case, the Negro's life can be seen, in Myrdal's terms, "as secondary reactions to more primary pressures from the side of the dominant white majority."[5] Thus, the black circus, early marching, and minstrel bands were an organized acceptance of Western forms, whereas the blues idiom and tradition can be seen as a rejection, or, at least, a reevaluation, of Western forms. Both traditions, however, are addressed directly to the American experience. The relationship between black and white America, often symbiotic, is nowhere more evident than in musical traditions.

The white minstrel tradition, which dates back to the early part of the nineteenth century at least, established that there was a *need* in white culture for what the black culture had to offer. It further suggested that white America preferred its doses of black culture in diluted form, just as the spiritual and field-holler showed that black America preferred to assimilate white culture in small doses. The rise of a black minstrel tradition was likewise a diluted form of black expression with a double twist: the black "cakewalk," for example, was an imitation of whites (white minstrels) imitating blacks imitating whites! The circus and minstrel bands were important not because they offered a showcase for black culture, but because they offered black musicians the opportunity to learn Western song forms, using Western instruments. If there was anything pathetic in the black minstrel tradition it was the emergence of an overtly white-oriented black secular music. This reflected the condition described by Fanon years later: "I begin to suffer from not being a white man to the degree that the white man imposes discrimination on me. . . . Then I will quite simply try to make myself 'white,' that is, I will compel the white man to acknowledge that I am human."[6] The rise of a black music employing Western instrumentation parallels the acceptance and facility with which the second and third generation Negroes were approaching the English language in general. Learning how to converse in Western idioms predicated the rise of a peculiarly black "American" tradition.

Jazz music, a result of the combination of the circus and minstrel bands with the blues tradition, is, strictly speaking, the urban voice of the black culture. In the process of urbanization, the rural blues musician met the organized band musicians, and the result is what we have come to recognize as early jazz. This is not to say that jazz is alien to rural areas and rural musicians but that increasing mobility and the rise of the recording industry in the first part of the twentieth century virtually brought the urban environment into rural life. Also, the general cultural flow of black Americans, beginning with the Great Exodus of 1879, is toward the urban areas. Jazz is a product of a peculiarly black voice (blues) in a peculiarly white context (Western harmony), and the result is a generally urban idiom. It is interesting to note that jazz is popular among South African blacks who have been exposed to and vilified by Western culture, but is virtually absent in West Africa where there is little Anglo-conformity, and an idiom known as "high life" is played to the exclusion of jazz. The necessity of white forms for the production of jazz music is clear, and the process of urbanization exposed more Negroes to these forms than ever before. Whereas black minstrelsy was an acceptance and an imitation of white modes, jazz—and the blues idiom upon which it was based—was an assimilation of these modes. Jazz has come to compose a tradition where it is not uncommon— indeed, it is always necessary, if sometimes at one or two removes—for whites to imitate blacks. This basic reversal of formative patterns is significant and, if understood, helps clear up some of the confusion surrounding modern activism in the American society, both white and black. Black culture is, above all, a culture that stresses actions, deeds not words; indeed, to accept black modes of expression is to embrace a kind of activism, in and of itself. This activism, which is part of the oral tradition, did not affect white cultures outside of America, nor did it take hold in white America until after the first generation. It was, however, preserved in the blues tradition.

The blues idiom is first and foremost a vehicle for individual expression, and its structure is perfectly suited to improvisation and spontaneous composition. It employs a minimum number of Western chords, and even these are in such a relation to one another as to allow the imposition of almost any note upon any chord. This allowed, the Afro-American tradition came to dominate the Western harmonic structure—a tradition of superimposed horizontal lines, which resembles harmony but is unlike true harmony in the Western sense inasmuch as the lines are relative to a tonic key (the dominant note of the scale) rather than to a series of chords. The result has been called "heterophonic" playing. Originally, the blues was a highly vocalized music which may have consisted "merely in the singing, over a steady, percussive rhythm, of lines of variable length, the length being determined by what phrase the singer had in mind, with equally variable pauses (the accompanying rhythm continuing) determined by how long it took the singer to think up another phrase."[7] The definition of the blues as a 12-bar, 3-lined form occurred around the turn of the century. It was necessary to the organized urban bands that took up the form and needed a more coherent structure but was ignored until well into the 1930s by country bluesmen. And yet survivors of the era claim that "the blues" was around long before they were. Like the term *jazz*, *blues* has come to mean many things to many people. The ability of this music to evade definition attests to its strength and survival power. One of the older blues players, Leadbelly, has given perhaps the most viable, nonanalytic definition: "The blues is a feeling and when it hits you, it's the real news."[8] This definition is particularly nice in that, since the blues does have the quality of never growing old, it is *always* "news." It is a form of expression that combines the immediacy of speech with the passion of song. As long as the blues continues to be the wellspring of black music, improvisation will be a vital element of the oral culture.

The blues form changes with fashion. It originated with a minimal number of chords, progressed through a welter of chord substitutions, and is currently employing the minimum number once again. The content of the blues changes necessarily with the times. Yet there is something permanent about the blues idiom, again, a *feeling* that can be likened to a positive, or creative, cynicism. Typified in the lyric, "I don't worry about a thing 'cause I know nothing's going to be all right," this cynicism is a matter of both tone and rhetoric. Inherent in this lyric, however, is an obvious affirmation. Perhaps there is the feeling that although things are bad, there is still no reason not to feel good. What is ultimately suggested is a basic belief in human organization, not excluding that form of organization the blacks had come to know: America. In this sense, even the poorest Negro exhibited the profoundest faith in what the American democracy stood for and believed that it was more than a hollow promise. The cynicism is closer to black humor than morbidity and grows out of the Love/Hate relationship Negroes have always had with America. As Harold Isaacs put it, "The deep and abiding identification of Negroes with America has had to persist in the face of the society's deep and abiding refusal to identify itself with Negroes."[9] The real danger of this relationship is not material but spiritual, not violence but the potential of the Negro to become disenchanted once and for all. The more widespread this potential for alienation is, the better it is articulated. Black musicians have not only given voice to the frustration of American Negroes, but they have created a channel for its release, and therein lies their great importance. Black music can resolve as well as generate tension of a specifically social nature. Because the two Americas are not mutually exclusive but exist in a relationship that creates a social atmosphere, the Anglo-conformity of American life is, although often inadvertently, a "racist climate." Anglo-conformity *implies* the ostensibly "necessary" subjugation of black values to white ways. Black cynicism, then, is a combination of the kind of faith in Justice practiced in black churches and the resentment which breeds in this climate, and which could have come only after the first secular failure of any proportion: Reconstruction. Prior to the late nineteenth century, the black culture did not have the "worldly cynicism" to sing the blues.

Blues, the secular "devil music," was both a catharsis for the anxieties caused by irrational suppression and, finally, a healthy, if cynical, assertion of the black ego. The pain of catharsis and the joy of assertion are not inconsistent and are both resolved in the blues. The cry and rhythmic freedom of the blues were transferred to Western instruments in the urbanization of black music. Today, jazz is not the only black idiom to employ these influences, but what can be allowed into the category *jazz* covers almost all blues music at the turn of the century. The "cry" was the trademark of the rural individual, derived from the Arwhollies, or field-hollers, and the vocalizations of the spirituals. It signaled that the individual was feeling in such-and-such a way, that he was alive and present, and that he was black. Just as middle-class Negroes shunned the poorer, more rural blacks because of their "heathen ways," they would likewise ridicule this "cry." Listeners would say, "Here comes Sam" or "Will Jackson's coming down the road" or "I just heard Archie down the road."[10] The "cry" would also be used as a release of tension, emitted when the individual was alone and out-of-hearing range. Blues melody derives its peculiar quality from the characteristics of the "cry," and the "blue notes" are not notes so much as basic vocalizations played on Western instruments.

It was necessary for the black ego to express itself in economic terms, particularly in an industrial, urban economy. "In a capitalistic society, economic wealth is inextricably interwoven with manhood. Closely allied is power—power to control and direct other men, power to influence the course of one's own and other lives."[11] Hence, the black musician has proceeded to take an aggressive stand in the realm of economics. Because of segregation, this has necessitated the establishment of a peculiarly black economic system. Musicians, gamblers, and hustlers of all kinds have been part of this system. The emergence of black economics was, in part, caused by the failure of white economics to provide a place for black culture and, as such, is further evidence of the inherent divisiveness in American culture. James Conant calls the irrational base of this divisiveness America's "congenital defect." The black culture could not turn to white economics for support but could survive only if supported by black economics. Further, it is well known that the "culture" which white America chooses as representative of the black population is not always that chosen by dominant black sentiment. The continued spiritual and financial support given to black musicians by the black culture at large indicates that these men should not be viewed as cultural deviants, as is generally the case, but rather should be considered cultural archetypes. Keil, defining black music as "ritual, drama, or dialectical catharsis," sees the black musician along with the black hustler as "ideal types representing two important value orientations for the lower-class Negro and need not be distinguished from the lower class as a whole. Both the hustler and the entertainer are seen as men who are clever and talented enough to be financially well-off without working."[12]

Although Keil recognizes from the socioeconomics of black life that the musician is a "cultural hero," he does not go on to point out that the very act of recognizing the musician as such is to establish a unique definition of work and play within the American context. It is not only that the black community does not view the underworld denizen as bad—there was precedent for that in the Devil figure in slave Christianity—but that the whole notion of a man's work as being separate and apart from a man's life is thrown into the air by the acceptance of these men as archetypes. Work, in the traditional sense, became equated with being within the realm of white economics, with working for the white man. This is not surprising, considering that many of the jobs the ex-slaves were forced to take made slavery look good.[13] Even today, black musicians call their day jobs "a slave." Work within the world of black culture, however, was quite a different proposition: a musician's work *is* his play. The part-time musician of the late nineteenth century began to approach this ethic, and the black musician-turned-professional of the early twentieth century caused a substantial revolution in value orientations within the black community. Somewhat in contrast to the tenets of Western Puritan tradition and to the demands of industrial society, the black culture was defining work as pleasure rather than as service, duty, or obligation. The black musician's *need* to play was internal rather than externally imposed, and this added to his status a kind of religious spiritualism. Whereas the hustler was "getting by," the musician was taking upon himself the socioeconomic role of the church. Black society encouraged the musician to obey his own dictates, while at the same time it made demands upon him which were not inconsistent with his own. Indeed, in the case of musicians within black culture, there is little distinction between personal and social motivation.

The legendary figure of Buddy Bolden can serve as a good

example of the early black professional musician. Born in 1868, Bolden was a transitional figure in the merging of the band tradition with the blues idiom. Growing up in an environment of Napoleonic brass marching bands, he played a Western instrument, the cornet, yet he knew well the African drum rituals of New Orleans' Congo Square. In 1896, he organized the first recognizable "jazz band"; in 1907, he ran amok during a parade and was committed to the State Hospital at Angola where he died twenty-four years later. Although many black musicians played Western instruments by this period, it was the *manner* in which Bolden approached the instrument that made him such an important transitional figure and gave the music he played the right to be called *jazz*. One of the surviving members of this first jazz band has said, "Now here is the thing that made King Bolden's Band the first to play jazz. It was because they could not read at all."[14] Bolden's conception was to use the instrument as an extension of the human voice. Since he did not read music, he had to rely solely on oral techniques. In fact, he employed Western forms and Western instrumentation to further these oral techniques. Still, he was able to "execute like hell and play in any key." Although he used many forms of Western music—the marches, quadrilles, and rags—he primarily played "blues of all kinds." These instrumental blues were really the major contribution of Bolden as a musician. So-called dirt music (the low, funky music of the "yard and field" Negroes) was his specialty, and whether he played in Tin Type Hall, a room used as a morgue by day and a dance hall by night, or at a church picnic, he played *loud*. Fred Ramsey suggests that the term *loud* to describe Bolden's playing by those who actually heard him may be a way of saying that the music as a whole was rough and unfamiliar—with "hoarseness, a notable lack of harmony, and a high level of heterophone"—in other words, a way of describing *"a new way of playing."*[15]

The effect this music had on the black culture was striking. One Negro of the period claims he left home at the age of fourteen after Bolden's band came through town: "I said, 'I'm going to New Orleans.' I had never heard anything like that before in my whole life."[16] A black musician who heard Bolden described the experience in almost identical terms: "I'd never heard anything like that before. I'd played 'legitimate' stuff. But this! It was somethin' that pulled me! . . . After that, I didn't play 'legitimate' so much."[17] Bolden himself occupied a very visible position in the community. "He was crazy for wine and women and vice versa. Sometimes he would have to run away from the women." Children fought to carry his horn, and the relationship between Bolden and the black community in general was that of "the King" and his spiritual "children." Bolden attended church where he clearly learned the foundations of "devil music," the vocalized tone and rhythms that, "when they got going would cross three times at once." His music was a synthesis of the pure African music of Congo Square, Western song form, and Afro-American church music. He was the first professional musician to stand head and shoulders above the others and exert his personal influence on the direction of black music. The synthesis of work and play, which he came to express, drove Bolden insane, however, because he had pioneered in an area in which psychological and sociological limits were not known. The oral, unlike the literate, tradition imposed no restraints on emotional excess. Bolden stayed up two and three nights at a time, drinking, playing, and "jiving" his women. "He was," says Louis Armstrong, "just a one man genius that was ahead of them all . . . too good for his time."[18]

If he was "too good for his time," his time and place were yet propitious to the rise of the new professional black musician. The question as to whether or not these musicians were consciously becoming professionals of a new order, different from the minstrel and circus band professionals, hinges on whether or not they were consciously playing a new kind of music for a specific audience. It is safe to say that, to some extent, the early New Orleans musicians were aware of their unique position in black history and exploited it to the full. The major difference between these musicians and the previous black professionals was the extent to which the new players were concerned with developing a peculiarly black sensibility, ignoring for the most part the white value structure to which the circus and minstrel players were attached. This was partly due to the fact that the circus and minstrel bands had to travel to make a living and hence never formed a clear understanding of the depths of local sentiment, while the New Orleans musicians were responsible solely to one city and to the social process of the people of that city.

New Orleans at the turn of the century was an urban environment of a peculiar character. It had developed into an important seaport, serving the inland states of the South and West, and it was undergoing a financial boom. Unlike the rest of the South, New Orleans had been a French colony before it joined the Union, and its French character remained throughout the nineteenth century. But perhaps most significant was the fact that the black population did not have to migrate to the urban center of New Orleans. Thus, New Orleans is not only the first urban "test case" for a uniquely black culture—one which would shape black socialization in Northern ghettos—but a truly urban home. The insecurity of rural life was counteracted by the security found in numbers, the financial prosperity, and the discovery of a singularly black social style. Black families had been dismembered during slavery and, to this day, the dominant family institution as the West knows it has never returned to the black community. New Orleans, however, provided the basis for the "extended family" system of black culture, the notion that still flourishes of black "brotherhood" based on socioeconomic lines rather than blood lines. Today, the term *blood* in street jargon means roughly the same thing as "brother," and "home boy" is still the name given to a newly arrived Southerner in the ghettos of the North. An examination of New Orleans becomes therefore an examination of the roots of modern black socialization.

The music profession during the first decade of the twentieth century was a cause for mixed emotions. Indeed, the black music of the period was in such a transitional state that in a few short years it progressed from an avocation to a full-fledged industry. This period of transition was characterized, on the one hand, by persistent aspirations toward white legitimacy. Although hope had been dashed by legal segregation, sentiment was still strong enough so that the "folks," in the words of a middle-class Creole, ". . . never had the idea they wanted a musician in the family." On the other hand, being a musician was the most natural goal for a black child: "[the kids] turned to what they saw and knew. Or if they were thick in the head, they'd end up doing stevedore work on the levee in the hot sun."[19] The two major industries—the job opportunities to which black children were exposed—were the work of the shipping yards and the play of the musicians and hustlers. And, too, because of the economic boom and the dance halls it brought, music was everywhere in the atmosphere of New Orleans. The Tenderloin District, where "the doors were taken off saloons from one year to the next" and "hundreds of men were passing through the streets day and night," became the center for commercialized black music. Equally important was the more general social aspect of music. The bands played for any occasion, and music was a strong social catalyst; indeed, it was included in all activities of black culture. "One of my pleasantest memories," recalls a Negro who was drawn as a child into the music business, ". . . was how a bunch of us kids playing would suddenly hear sounds. It was like a phenomenon, like the Aurora Borealis—maybe. The sounds of men playing would be so clear. . . . The city was full of the sounds of music."[20]

Ultimately, musical expression became a legitimate "occupation" for the black youngster, and much, if not all, of the taint of musicianship on a professional level was lost. "From the age of seven, my Mother had stressed the importance of knowledge and a profession to keep from being the white man's lackey. So she insisted I take music lessons."[21] This statement, made in reference to the period following the New Orleans experience, typifies the resolution of the conflict surrounding black music as a business. And if it was necessary for the black ego to express itself in financial terms, at least these terms were decided upon by the black community at large. In New Orleans, Negroes discovered one another through competition of all kinds. Any activity became grounds for testing the personal or economic strength of one Negro against another. "Everybody in New Orleans—for it was a very competitive city—had the reputation for doing something best."[22] The individuation within black music, the necessity for each man to have his own "sound," tended to ease this competitive pressure by enabling more people to "do well"; there was no narrow category of good music or good performance. The importance of the individual was second to that of the group in New Orleans, yet this period can be seen as the beginning of a trend, which parallels that of urbanization, wherein the group sentiment is more often than not shaped by individual innovation. The urban environment encouraged the individual psychologically to stretch out much further than had been allowed in rural society. As Morris has recognized, "Only in the city does sustained innovation stand a real chance. Only the city is strong enough and secure enough in its amassed conformity to tolerate the disruptive forces of rebellious originality and creativity."[23] To showcase the positive aspects of blackness, originality and improvisation were placed in an economic context through the competitive atmosphere of the "carving contest": "Down the street, in an old sideboard wagon, would come the jazz band from one ballroom. And up the street, in another sideboard wagon, would come the band from another ballroom, which had announced a dance for the same night at the same price. And those musicians played for all their worth, because the band that pleased the crowd more would be the one the whole crowd would go to hear."[24]

Music was not a full-time profession for more than a handful of black musicians in the early days of New Orleans, but it was part of the larger gaming industry of the city. In fact, "the hustlers, gamblers, and racetrack followers were often hard-working musicians in their off seasons, or when their luck turned and they needed a little ready cash."[25] Money made from playing was considered "fun money" and was poured back into the gambling economy. Gambling is particularly attractive to the very rich and the very poor but anathema to the middle-class. Thus, New Orleans society was poison to the middle-class mentality. The rise of a peculiarly black professional ethic, then, was in part due to the destruction of middle-class mentality by black musicians. Prior to the segregation law of 1894, a great colored middle-class had flourished among the Creoles, the *gens de couleur* of French, Spanish, and African blood. This caste had achieved a precarious position of legitimacy within the white world. With the discrimination code of 1894, these wealthy Creoles were forced to return with their advanced musical knowledge to the mainstream of black culture or were left to nurture the false hope that they would be restored to their old position within white society. The kind of adaptation to white values they had practiced, and that had been at the very foundation of their training, was no longer possible. These Creoles were either assimilated into black culture or suffered what Ellison has called "invisibility." One Creole musician recalls that "us Downtown people, we didn't think so much of this rough Uptown jazz until we couldn't make a living otherwise. . . . If I wanted to make a living, I had to be rowdy like the other group. I had to jazz it or rag it or any other damn thing. . . . Bolden caused all that . . . can't tell you what's there on the paper, but just play the hell out of it."[26] Thus ended, the overt battle for white legitimacy in New Orleans became, within the oral tradition, a fight for position next to men like Bolden; in the long run, this process had a solidifying effect on black culture.

There are several reasons why the black culture was strengthened by the Creole culture. First, the Creoles brought a valuable infusion of knowledge that shaped the nature of black music, the harmonic and melodic structure of the more sensual Latin music and the more "exotic" $\frac{2}{4}$ and $\frac{6}{8}$ time signatures of the quadrilles. The romanticism of this Latin music opened the way for black musicians to move comfortably into the world of popular music. In the twentieth century, Negroes have dominated in the interpretation of Western song form, particularly the 32-bar Tin Pan Alley construction. Although there was some precedent for this in the early slave "ballits," the exposure to Latin music was the source of a black *ballad* tradition, love songs that employ Western song form rather than blues structure but that retain the emotional content of blues playing. The $\frac{2}{4}$ and $\frac{6}{8}$ signatures of the quadrille, as well as the $\frac{4}{4}$ feel of the Napoleonic marching bands, proved to be good foundations for the imposition of the more complex African rhythms found in Congo Square. Second, the infusion of Creole knowledge allowed the black culture to address itself with more confidence to the monolithic Anglo-conformity of Western culture. It added information without which the black culture could not gauge its true relationship to white culture, and in so doing, it galvanized the strength of the black position. The desire for white legitimacy remained but became more covert, paralleling the Booker T. Washington theory that "progress" would come through contributions to Western markets. Finally, the Creoles brought with them a kind of professional attitude toward music that was unknown in black culture. Blues music had been private, personal, and very informal. The Negro circus and minstrel musicians had given the black culture a small taste of the entertainment ethic, but the black professional musician who was not only an instrumentalist but also an *entertainer* did not emerge until after the Creole infusion (formal entertainment was "unnecessary" to the isolated lower-class Negroes).

French culture and the presence of Catholicism provided a climate of "cultural laissez-faire" that allowed the perpetuation of overt Africanisms, killed elsewhere by the harsher Anglo-Protestant ethic. Because the Latin-Catholic planter "didn't seem to care what a slave thought or did in his spare time," the *vodun* rituals of the Dahomean tribe, normally private, got a continuous public airing in Congo Square until the Square itself was demolished in 1885.[27] The *vodun* cults were a major source of social organization and owe their survival power, in part, to the syncretism of their gods and Catholic saints. The importance of these cults is enormous and lies not only in the fact that *vodun* ritual was a great reservoir of rhythm in black spiritualism. *Vodun* was not a secular tradition, but it was not a Christian tradition, either. Unlike Christianity, it did not put the spirit above the flesh but maintained the two on an equally exalted level, established through the use of music, particularly its rhythmic aspects. The act of playing music in these rituals went along with the act of prayer. As *vodun* became a highly popular, if secret, religion throughout the Louisiana area, and, indeed, throughout the South as a whole, it spread the exalted function of black music. It was a version of "spirit possession" that made even the more enthusiastic black churches appear tame, and group catharsis reached its uppermost limit in these rituals. If black musicians gained professionalism from the middle-class traditions, they clearly received a stage presence from both *vodun* and Christian music. In religious ritual, members would be in various stages of advanced "possession" yet would at all times be responsive to the ritual as a whole. As Herskovitz has pointed out, "possession" is "for all its hysterical quality, by no means undisciplined."[28] The ability to perform music at the peak of emotional involvement, to be able to maintain the pitch of this involvement, and continue the process of spontaneous composition separates black entertainment from almost all of Western tradition. This stage presence, which accounts for the impact of the black personality on the entertainment industry in general and the music industry specifically, is reinforced in black churches even today, but the importance of *vodun* as a non-Christian source of inspiration is significant in that it foreshadows the rise of a black secular music that was nonetheless spiritually oriented.

The standard interpretation of New Orleans jazz is that it came out of a basically hedonistic society. I disagree strongly with this view because it seems evident, both from what we know of black history and from the musical artifacts of this period, that black music was very much spiritually inclined. It was even perhaps a secular manipulation of Christian tradition and it relied heavily on the notion of a group "spirit," an almost tangible mutuality. The close-knit quality of black society was present in the ensemble type of collective, or group, improvisation that flourished when jazz was not yet a full-time, occupationally competitive profession There were, strictly speaking, no soloists, and although different men altered the direction of the music, the individual musician was showcased only during the "breaks" he took at the end of a chorus. Indeed, the notion of a *group sound* was so dominant that drummers would try to play their instruments "in tune" with the rest of the group, no small achievement. Baby Dodds, who was especially noted for his ability to do this, has said of his own approach, ". . . *drumming is spirit.* . . . You got to have that in your body, in your soul. . . . And it can't be an evil spirit. . . . If you're evil, you're going to drum evil, and if you drum evil, you're going to put evil in somebody else's mind."[29] Hence, one can hear in the early New Orleans music a kind of secular spirituality, based on the involvement and integrity of the individual but possible only through group action. In its strongest form, this meant physical participation by all concerned. The audience was a dancing audience from the beginning of jazz music. In a sense, the music of New Orleans was created by both the performer and the audience in a constant interaction, an exchange of faith, not unlike that of the preacher-congregation relationship or that of *vodun* ritual.

The rhythmic feeling of the earliest marching bands had its "swing" or "syncopation" not from the alteration of Western time signatures but from the imposition of African-type rhythms on these signatures. The great African drums of *vodun* ritual were replaced by the bass drums of the marching band, and the men who played them, like Black Benny, were famous for their ability to move a whole band with a single drum and an "African" beat. In the first years of the century, these marching bands formed around the numerous secret societies. The integration of music and social activity in the secret societies was not covert, and was thus less radical than that of *vodun*. These secret societies were modeled in part on the traditional white lodges and fraternal orders, in part on the white secret organizations such as the Ku Klux Klan that began as social organizations but had ulterior purposes. Primarily, the secret society was a unit of lower-class organization, a secular substitute for the kind of structure the church alone had provided earlier. Established "to furnish pastime from the monotony of work, a field of ambition, and intrigue, a chance for parade and insurance against misfortune,"[30] the society consisted of anywhere from several to several hundred men and women who joined together and contributed money toward picnics, parades, burial expenses, and, not incidentally, the maintenance of a marching band. The musicians accompanied the members on all outings and received little financial compensation. A major difference between the Creole musician and his marching band counterpart was that the Creole's music was more an economic activity—a difference that can be thought of as both social precept and attitude of style.

The function of the funeral and the role of the musician at the funeral, for example, were typical of the peculiarly black *style* of social organization. "A woman's got to belong to at least seven secret lodges if she 'spects to get buried with any style," said one woman of the period. "And the more lodges you belongs to, the more music you gits when you goes to meet your maker. . . . I'm sure lookin' forward to my wake. They is wakin' me for four nights and I is gonna have the biggest funeral the church ever had. That's why everythin' I make goes to . . . them societies."[31] There are hints of ancestor worship in this account, like the basic African conception of the survival of the spirit after death, and hints too of a kind of hopelessness of the worldly life. It is clear, however, that the musician was well integrated into the life and death—the daily round—of the lower-class Negro and thus into the economic foundations of that life. During the funerals, the musician provided something like a spiritual soundtrack for the proceedings. The drummers played slow, grim funeral time on the way to the cemetery. However, as the service at the grave was ending, it was the drummer's job to start the parade back to the lodge for the party. A good drummer, who knew the best moment to make the most dramatic effect, could snap the crowd completely out of mourning. "We would have a second line back—all in the street, all on the sidewalk, in front of the band, and behind the lodge, in front of the lodge. We'd have some immense crowds following. They would follow the funeral to the cemetery just to get this ragtime music comin' back."[32]

However, as the job market in New Orleans grew, these men spent more time working in dance halls and less time in the street parades. It has been noted that only through his economic position could the black musician initially rise above the average member of the black community and provide leadership, however informal. The creation of a commercial area specifically set aside for black music, such as the dance hall, was a major step in making black music more "legitimate," as well as a contributing factor in the elevation of the black musician's status. T. Bone Walker has noted, "The first blues I heard was my mother singing about dinner burning or anything like that. I guess that obscenity was built up with commercial playing of the blues."[33] When the blues became commercial property, the bluesman became a member of the business world. The Negro, then, became "Americanized" when he played the blues for money. The economic rewards were seldom commensurate with his talents or with the white norms; still, the black musician was almost solely responsible for dragging the black culture into an assertive posture within the marketplace of the white world.

The financial factor, however, was also a cause for the further separation of white and black America if only because of the disparity between the acceptance by white musicians of black music and the lack of acceptance by white audiences of the black musician himself. The New Orleans Negroes "felt very highly about what they were playing, as though they knew they were doing something new that nobody else could do."[34] Yet the first large financial gains were made by white musicians playing black music to essentially white audiences. Many of these white musicians got their musical education in the "second line" of the black marching bands and admittedly tried to play as much like the black originators as possible. White musicians have traditionally shown a great regard for black innovators and have often achieved a great empathy with black culture. The incidence of racism, as distinct from race consciousness, has always been low among white jazzmen, and, at some level, even the most casual white record enthusiast has accepted something of the black attitude. The general white audience, however, has preferred the white imitation to the black original almost every time. This was substantiated perhaps for the first time with the success of the white "Original Dixieland Jazz Band" at Reisenweber's Cabaret in New York during 1917. This band, fresh from New Orleans, provided the general public with its first opportunity to hear black music, and because they made the first recordings of out-and-out jazz that sold by the millions, introduced the word *jazz* into the white vocabulary and created an overnight sensation. I think it very doubtful that any black group during this period could have had that kind of impact on white America; perhaps the success of the Original Dixieland Jazz Band proves this, for they were certainly not the best men out of New Orleans and, within several years, were playing commercial, non-jazz music to a middle-brow crowd.

Yet the success of this band and the fact that an all-white band openly paid allegiance to the black culture seem to me to open a new phase in the historical relationship between black and white America. On the one hand, it was obvious that whites found much that was attractive, even necessary, within black music, and learning black idioms of expression, like learning another man's language, was basically an act of respect and friendship on the part of white musicians. At the same time, it was an indication of a growing disaffection within the white community with white norms. One fairly recent study by psychologist Norman Margolis recognizes this relationship between jazz idioms and social protest. This may be especially true in the case of white musicians. Margolis writes that "as jazz progressed out of the specific areas of its birth, it ran into the American culture which places a high value on properness, control and restraint. In other words the general Puritan, Anglo-Saxon tradition, by this time solid in this country, dictated a rigid cultural conscience which required the repression of the objectionable impulses with which jazz had become associated and symbolized."[35] White players were perhaps conscious of the "protest" value of black music as early as minstrelsy. And black musicians certainly have never been unaware of this element of their music. At the same time, however, I doubt that their music has been motivated by a dominant *protest* sentiment. More basically, their music was an assertion of the oral orientation. In Jones's phrase, for example, Louis Armstrong "was, in terms of emotional archetypes, an honored priest of his culture, one of the most impressive products of his society. Armstrong was not *rebelling* against anything with his music."[36] Two points emerge here that are worth mentioning because they remain central to the discussion of black music in America: first, that the black musician has, himself, been the *product* in the music business, and that although his music is often accepted, his person is invariably exploited; second, that the black musician has constantly had to maneuver around psychological misunderstandings, often very subtle ones, that surround his music in order to present that music to mainstream America, to all Americans, as a statement that speaks for itself.

3 🎵

The Jazz Age:
The 1920s

The 1920s, first called the "Jazz Age" by F. Scott Fitz-
gerald, was a period of affluence, escapism, and extensive
cross-cultural activity for many Americans. It was a complex
state of mind as well as an actual span of years. This state
of mind altered the feeling of life in both black and white
America, as well as the course of American history. The
decade was peculiar in that, for the first time, the music of
the black culture—and "vulgar" culture in general—became
part of mainstream American expression. This acceptance of
vulgar idioms not only tended to break down the old Western
categories of Art and Life, pulling the Artist out of his ivory
tower and into the onrushing stream of History, but also
romanticized the role of the black musician. Although this
romanticism was reflected in the music of many young white
musicians, it was the black musicians who remained faithful
to the techniques of expression peculiar to the oral culture.
As I have suggested, these techniques stem from neither
romanticized nor idealized views of the world but, as exemplified by the blues, are founded and rooted in great realism.
The complexity of the "Jazz Age" can be seen in the assimilative trends of the decade—the meeting of the currents of
black and white American culture—which were based on
subtle misconceptions, both social and psychological. One as-
piring white jazz critic wrote in 1925, "The true spirit of

jazz is a joyous revolt from convention, custom, authority, boredom, even sorrow—from everything that would confine the soul of man and hinder its riding free on the air. . . . And that is why it has become such a balm for modern ennui, and has become a safety valve for modern machine-ridden and convention-bound society. It is the revolt of the emotions against repression."[1] Although there is some truth in this, there is also a subtle misconception: that the Negro in America is basically naive, a cultural primitive, and has therefore maintained à kind of escapist innocence in the face of technology. As I have attempted to stress, the black man in America *appears* primitive to Western man, but the assertion of an oral orientation is not so much *anti*-technology as it is, basically, and in approach, *non*-technology. The misconceptions that arose in the twenties, then, were due partly to general ignorance of black tradition and partly to wish-fulfillment and projection-of-self by the white culture. At the same time, black musicians were attaining a new position of respectability within white society and were, to varying extents, willing to perpetuate the white misconceptions and make accommodations to traditional Western criteria. The flow of black and white culture in America can be seen as crosscurrents which, though joined temporarily during the twenties, were undeniably headed in different directions.

Hence the image of black culture held by whites was often incongruent with the self-image of black Americans. Basically, the motivations for the white acceptance of black music were at odds with the motivations that created the music. Whites gravitated toward black music and black culture in general because they felt it expressed the abandon and hedonism toward which they liked to think they were moving. Indeed, the "Jazz Age" was characterized by its selfconscious attempt at appearing unselfconscious, its sophisticated awareness of the advantages of an unsophisticated approach, and its growing awareness of the body of international opinion, which ran roughshod over the rigid prewar Victorian sensibility (in America, this had been predicated upon a kind of cultural isolationism). The new "Jazz Age" sensibility and the affluence from which it came seemed to amplify the acquisitive instinct of all Americans: Americans in large numbers not only had money to spend but even the middle-class seemed eager to spend it for the pleasure of spending or to "get rich quick." Indeed, this fiscal attitude, tangential to the dissolution of nineteenth-century rationalism, contributed to the collapse of the stock market by 1929. Americans, as consumers, developed a love for *newness* (perhaps originally part of the pioneering ethic but not to be confused with an innovative spirit), for *bigness* (a result, possibly, of the influence of assembly-line techniques and mass production), and for materialism of a high order. This essentially white (Western) value structure that came out of the 1920s suggested an American who loved to *have* things rather than one who had things to love. Although this is a caricaturization, an oversimplification of mainstream American life, it is faithful to the spiritual vacuity that, enveloping the postwar American, seemed to be a natural consequence of the collapse of prewar idealism and moral fervor. Heightened materialism, however, seemed to stimulate a need for its opposite—spirituality—that was conspicuous by its very absence. This need for an other-worldliness to counterbalance the increasingly materialistic orientation of life was evident in the rise of a parlor-room and essentially middle-class variety of "witchcraft." These rather low-camp séances acted as a spiritual placebo and gave a faddish, fashion-conscious aspect to the decade. But the introduction of black music into the American experience, although it was at times packaged and marketed in a tepid Tin Pan Alley form, indicated a need for, and a recognition of, a spiritualistic element of a much higher order. In times of heightened materialism, emotional honesty takes on a revolutionary aura and appears as an overt alternative to mainstream values. Black music can, and did, exist as a nonideological spiritual outlet, naturally evolved by the Negro and consciously adopted by whites. Again, the motivations that produced black music within the oral culture were of a more primary nature than those that made it an attractive outlet for whites.

In examining the motivations behind the white acceptance of black culture, one must take into account the rise of gangsterism in response to Prohibition. Gangsterism, although overtly illegal, was covertly approved of by many Americans because it had come to fill a need. In this sense, gangsterism was organized violence, to some extent publicly condoned, established to combat Federal legislation that many Americans felt to be repressive. Gangsterism not only enhanced the romanticism of the decade—Al Capone was legendary as well as notorious—but also tended to break down traditional definitions of cultural deviance. If organized violence was somehow legitimized by the fact that it fulfilled an emotional need in mainstream America, then it became possible for other previously considered deviant behavior patterns to be somewhat legitimized too. Practically overnight, the black musician became a symbol of the socially liberated American. This position was reinforced by the black musician's association, especially in Chicago, with the gangsters who ruled the nightlife. Because the black musician had grown up in the milieu of condoned, if unorganized, violence, he was moving in familiar psychological territory when he reached the street violence of Chicago. The white culture was perhaps as much impressed with his offhand acceptance of what normally would have been considered deviant behavior as it was with his music. This underworld flavor of his life became subject to social myth, and the spirit of resistance in his music became all the more relevant to whites. Gangsterism seemed to be an expression of spontaneous and highly physical social behavior, and the "Lost Generation" of the twenties found no better precedent for social improvisation than in the music and general orientation of black culture. Also, the live-it-first writing style of authors like Hemingway indicated that the white culture during the twenties had developed an indisposition toward social improvisation and that black music was filling an "unstimulated demand" by providing a physical outlet.

The general feeling of life in black America had responded to the promises of affluence that appeared to be the new trend. Certainly, the black worker in Northern industry was earning more than ever before—he was *gaining* on the whites, and this was a source of optimism—and the black musician in the North was no exception. The music industry began to pay extraordinary fees to top talent, and black musicians were eager to become part of this industry. On the other hand, black culture had also responded to the international consciousness of the twentieth century, and this consciousness tended to disrupt the tenuous alliance between black and white America. The victory of the off-color nation of Japan over the Russians in the Tsushima Strait was marked in the black community by the launching of the "Niagara movement" in 1906. This forerunner of the NAACP had as its goal the application of legal and political pressure to ensure better race relations. By the end of World War I, however, the spirit of accommodation within the lower-class black society had been eroded by some severe shocks. The eruption of Marcus Garvey's back-to-Africa movement, though patently unsuccessful in achieving its stated goals, was the first black social movement of any stature to express "black pride" in no uncertain terms. Garvey had progressed, with a base of mass support numbering in the millions, to a stage of militancy and disaffection unknown to Du Bois and his followers at the NAACP. He was quick to criticize the NAACP for its "lack of concern for the ordinary black." He accused the more legitimate organization of not personally *involving* lower-class Negroes and hinted that black people "have not forgotten the prowess of war."[2] If Garvey's policies were a reflection of the legitimized violence of the period, they were also the expression of a new race consciousness that was taking hold among the "ordinary" black men. As many as half a million black soldiers had fought in Europe during World War I and had experienced almost no racial prejudice while away from America. They returned not only distrustful of the rhetoric of American politicians, but also somewhat aware of a black "nationhood" submerged by Western traditions, but potentially strong enough to assert itself. Garvey himself indicated that "we of the UNIA [his organization] have studied seriously this question of nationality among Negroes—this American nationality . . . and have discovered that it counts for nought when that nationality comes in conflict with the racial idealism of the group that rules."[3] The ordinary, lower-class black man was becoming conscious, indeed, self-conscious, of being an *internal émigré* in America.

It would perhaps be a greater mistake to exaggerate Garvey's influence than it would be to minimize it. Garvey represented a politically conscious black movement. Other black movements, without formal leadership or considered policy, were not uncommon during this period. Indeed, race riots have never been more common than they were during and immediately following World War I. One example occurred after 60,000 Negroes migrated to Chicago from the South prior to 1920. With the migration, the climate grew increasingly tense. In July of 1919, a five-day race riot over the ostensible issues of police prejudice, labor relations, and unfair housing practices—precisely the issues the NAACP attempted to take to the courts—brought out the fact that the black culture was slowly losing its fear of direct social action. This riot was not a conscious application of militant techniques, as is modern ghetto warfare, but rather a spontaneous eruption of natural power caused by the strain of social frustrations. (It should be noted that the black culture did not seek to challenge and reject the Anglo-conformity of American life so much as it attempted to alter and integrate that philosophy with its own.) Negroes wanted "in" and were being held back because of cultural biases. Garvey's organization was mere pageantry and could not act as a social outlet for this frustration; riots were a more direct means of involving the common Negro. Yet even the riots indicated a kind of optimism that made the twenties an assimilatory era. First, the riots did *involve,* personally, large numbers of blacks, for the first time, in the process of urban decision-making. Secondly, they rarely sought other than integrationist goals. The general sentiment in the black community seemed to be that if the white man could be made to understand the nature and consequence of racial discrimination, better conditions would arise. The sad truth which became evident years later, was that the white man, from the very beginning of slavery, had chosen *not* to understand the nature and consequence of racial discrimination: that is, he understood them all too well. During the twenties, however, social action seemed predicated upon the belief that first, things were getting better and second, the Negro could actually *do* something to improve his situation and accelerate the arrival of a secular justice. The fatalism, the bitter nihilism of modern ghetto life was conspicuously missing.

As an outlet for black aggression, black music, as ritual, was perhaps somewhere between the extremes of pageantry and riot. The Negro's Love/Hate relationship with America was clearly expressed and underscored in the black music of the period. Black musicians used more and more Western song forms, incorporated Western harmony, and played for increasingly integrated audiences. The spread of jazz, particularly from the blues, into white society became a two-way prócess; black and white America began making cultural concessions to each other. Yet at the same time, a new aspect developed in the playing of the professional black musician: the importance of innovation as a means of keeping black musical idioms out of the hands of white imitators. In fact it was the case that no sooner had some whites learned the special techniques of black music than Negro musicians developed new, more difficult techniques to replace them. On the one hand, this was caused by the musician's new awareness of the economic value of his music, a fact brought home by the acceptance of his music by white society; on the other hand, the maintenance of purely and exclusively black idioms and techniques can be seen as "the drive for a unique and ethnically singular method of expression" within the black culture.[4] This suggests that, perhaps for reasons of self-preservation, the black culture, even while it was reaching out for the recognition of white society, sought to make a stand on its cultural uniqueness. Grier and Cobbs find this to be a deep psychological drive within the American Negro, one that cannot be separated from his social actions. Their suggestion is that the American Negro, subconsciously and perhaps contrary to his own overt aspirations, tends to flaunt the fact of his blackness in white America's collective face, in order to repudiate best white America's covert denigration of black culture in general. Black music in the twenties, then, became more overtly devious as it became accepted by whites. The ambiguous position of black culture—not yet ready to abandon either the strength of cultural isolation or the hope for assimilation —was an undeniable theme of the decade.

Although he was not the first New Orleans musician to reach Chicago, Louis Armstrong was most notable for the equipoise, the visceral balance between Western and Negro musical styles of his playing. Perhaps no one walked the fence between the two cultures better than he did. Like

Bolden before him, Armstrong was an innovator whose influence seemed single-handedly to reform black music. The balance of intellectual and emotional content in his playing impressed a vast and integrated audience. Armstrong combined the oral approach to rhythm and vocalization with an intuitive grasp of Western harmonic structure, creating a new synthesis acceptable to both blacks and whites. Even as a young man, Armstrong was unlike other trumpet players in the way he incorporated Western harmonies with the blues. One local musician recalled, "I was the 'Blues King' of New Orleans, and when Louis played that day he played more blues than I ever heard in my life. It never did strike my mind that blues could be interpreted so many different ways. Every time he played a chorus it was different and you knew it was blues."[5] The variety of Armstrong's blues was a result of the imposition of chord substitutions on the minimal blues format, not a strictly worked out assault on Western harmonic structure but an evolved, intuitive manipulation of what information was available to an "unschooled" musician. Although in later life he learned how to read music, his understanding of Western harmonic structure was originally a function of what he heard, of his ability to play "by ear" and "hear" the logic of harmonic structure at an often subconscious, or perhaps preconscious, level. Relying on the ability to read music implies a rigid *preconception* whereas playing "by ear" is part of the more free-flowing oral tradition and is merely *conception*. Hence, a musician can always learn to read music but, as is well known, even some of the best readers, i.e., the Western classical musicians, cannot "fake it," or improvise on a given body of material. One cannot be taught how to improvise black musical idioms, because the *theory* of improvisation develops through the *doing* of it. The act *is* the theory. Armstrong, it has been said, proved the idea that "if you can't sing it, you can't play it," that improvisation is based on the ability to "hear" with internal ears the sound of an internal voice. This reliance on "internal hearing" is part of the more general approach of the oral orientation, and indeed, Armstrong's horn playing sounded remarkably like his singing.

Armstrong's distinctly sophisticated—one could even say *rational*—version of the blues was almost fully developed before he reached Chicago where it came to fruition. His immigration to that city was part of the greater cultural migration of the period, part, too, of the general trend, which continues today, of blues innovation and techniques flowing from South to North. Armstrong's immigration and subsequent success became part of the black social legend wherein the "bad nigger" had to leave the South and prove his manhood in the North, a process finally reversed during the sixties when the "bad niggers" like Stokely Carmichael became the first generation to return to the South. Ironically, the Southern musicians not only had to deal with the education of white audiences in the North, but also had to reintegrate much of the black population into the oral tradition. Armstrong himself recalls his surprise at discovering the validity of this trend. "We watched close to see what their music would be like," he remembers of his first exposure to Northern Negro jazz musicians, "because we knew they had a big reputation in St. Louis and naturally, we were interested to see how our New Orleans bands, like Kid Ory's and the rest, would stack up against them. Well, we were surprised. In no time at all we could tell they were doing things that had been done down home years before. The leader would try to swing them away from the score but they didn't seem to know how."[6] The Northern blacks could read music, but they couldn't "swing away from the score" or "fake it." This ability relied on exposure to the oral tradition, which was diluted or altogether lacking in Northern cities. In areas of recent black migration, such as Chicago or Kansas City, the problem was not as severe as it was in St. Louis or New York, which had older, more established black communities. It can be suggested that this is the main reason why jazz "grew up" in Chicago and, later, Kansas City, but generally "passed through" New York and, to a lesser extent, St. Louis. In fact, the blues did not take root in New York until the late forties. Those areas with black populations fresh from the South drew their cultural security from Southern traditions; hence the importance of Chicago in the twenties.

The very context of Chicago generated new rules for black music and for black socialization. The music became more of a closely guarded, culturally exclusive property. Professional jealousy developed according to economic rather than artistic criteria as a higher commercial value was placed on the music. Freddie Keppard reacted by refusing to make records, although he was reputed to be one of the best of the Southern musicians and one of the first offered a recording opportunity, because he didn't want his music "stolen." "King" Oliver, who ultimately brought Armstrong up from the South and with whom Armstrong first recorded, had an elaborate system of signals worked out with his band to keep his improvisational techniques a secret from others; he would, for example, alter his playing when the "alligators" would take out their pens and pencils to copy down his music on napkins, tablecloths, and even shirt cuffs. This professional jealousy had a very subtle effect on black socialization. On the one hand, it seemed to stimulate and increase the importance of innovation, or, at least, of individuation, within a normally group-oriented society. On the other hand, this stress on the individual tended to alter slightly the warm, "extended family" pattern of socialization known in the South and to replace this greater group interrelation with smaller musical "in-groups" or "clans." This "in-grouping" is perhaps a central cause of the exoticism of black music in urban ghettos, as each "clan" attempts to outperform and surpass rival groups with ever bolder innovations. Later, this trend, which has its origin in the twenties, developed into full-fledged in-group hostility. As one black musician said recently, "You never want to let somebody out-hip you, because then you have to go convince everybody that it was your idea in the first place." This kind of in-group hostility was a result of the pressures generated by the entrance of black music into the white marketplace. Although at times in-group hostility has been an unfortunate consequence of black urbanization, it has also aided in the diversification of black music as it moved into the rarefied realms of twentieth-century Art.

Perhaps the most dramatic element in the shaping of black social relationships in the twenties was the recording industry itself. Born during the previous decade, the record industry had overwhelmed all America in just a few short years. By the middle of the twenties, homes that had neither electricity nor running water often had a phonograph. The effect of recordings on black socialization remains open to interpretation. The effects of various technologies are still not fully understood, as can be witnessed by the speculation today concerning the influence of the television industry,[7] but it seems apparent that records did more than just impart information. In some respects, records hold a relationship to music similar to that of the printing press to literature. Yet, recordings deal in aural rather than visual perception and thus reinforce the basic precepts of orality. The recording is not simply a documentary device that composes a new selective tradition—affecting who heard what when—but a means for reshaping and extending the oral tradition. I would suggest, for example, that recordings, in making a more or less permanent *object* of music, thus leaving it open to the kind of reconsideration and preconception that characterizes literacy, become subject to the critical interpretations surrounding any socially relevant source of information. That is, recording can politicize music, a theme particularly important during the fitties and sixties. The major influence of recordings during the twenties was in the spread of black music across almost all the previous geographic and social barriers. The black man in the South could listen to, learn from, and economically support the black musician in the North, just as the reverse was also, if less often, true. Many Negroes in all parts of the United States gained their first significant exposure to their own culture through records rather than through live performances. Billie Holiday, for example, ran errands for local prostitutes just to earn the privilege of listening to Louis Armstrong records. Also, records allowed black music to go where black musicians could not go. Certainly more than one white household was "integrated" through recordings of black music during this decade. Recordings also brought black music to the whites who were hesitant to frequent the living environment of black music. The recording industry predated by several years the influence of radio and was the major source of cross-cultural transmission during the early twenties.

The information content of recordings was, by definition, different from that of live music, not only because recording freezes the music and allows critical distance and preconception, but because the three-minute time limit of early acoustic and electric recordings (78 rpm's) curtailed the extended improvisation of black music.[8] Musicians were forced to encapsulate their ideas, prestructure their improvisation to the physical limits of the actual record, and aim their music at a technological rather than human source of feedback. Hence, musicians under recording circumstances developed a sense of abstraction, a new professional distance from their music. The small details of improvisation, which would normally have gone unnoticed, became available for afterthought: music took on a spatial aspect, wherein the length of the record (predetermined) was the distance the music could travel, and even the more vulgar idioms became subject to laws that characterize Art: *Art* being "inspired conception tempered with critical distance from the source of that inspiration." It is possible that without the recording industry, black music would have gone the way of all "folk" music and would not have developed into the sophisticated mode of cultural expression it is today. Black music became more complicated and urbane because of recording.

Through records, the relationship between the black musician and his audience was radically altered. Once so thoroughly mutual, this relationship became, with the recording industry, one-sided: the musician performed and the listener received, could even dance to, but could not affect in any way—short of choosing or not choosing to buy the record—the content or quality of that music. Thus the performer/audience relationship was all the more reduced to economic terms. This forced the audience to a certain extent to *come* to black music; they had to be consciously *prepared* for it and/or subconsciously approve of its effects. The black musician tended to become more experimental in the recording studio, not only because there could be "retakes," second efforts previously irrelevant to the improvisation process, but also because he was forced to rely on his own musical sense to decide whether the record was "good enough." The critical sense of the musician was generally more advanced, more open perhaps, than that of the average listener. Of course, the opposite was also the case: recordings often forced the musician to be less experimental, either because he feared he would make "a mistake" or because some recording executive would dictate aesthetic criteria to him. In both these cases, which were a matter of record company policy as well as the effects of technology, musicians were allowed to reconsider their music, and, equally important, the audience was allowed a more cerebral approach. This was particularly useful to young whites who were attracted to the music but had no cultural precedents to bring to bear on its improvisation. Recorded jazz lent itself to analysis, to being reduced to simple constituent parts and reassembled; in short, to being *learned*. The members of the white Austin High gang, a group of Chicago teen-agers who went on to become serious jazz musicians, learned to play their instruments by stopping and starting jazz records and memorizing, note for note, the music of the New Orleans Rhythm Kings, ironically a white group that imitated the "colored style." The Austin High gang, in fact, worked their first professional jobs as jazz musicians before they were able to improvise.

This points again to a disparity between the white attraction toward black music, which was natural enough, and the extent of their empathy with the modes of black culture, which was invariably forced. Traditionally, black music developed out of techniques invented by black musicians randomly and for the sole purpose of individualized expression. The technique developed *out of* the feeling of the moment. This emotional honesty was what had initially attracted the Austin High gang to black music: "That was what we believed, in the Austin gang in Chicago," said one of its members, "play the way you feel, yourself!" The techniques of jazz playing, however, and hence the feel of jazz music are inescapably a function of the social orientation of the individual musician. Thus, a black self-taught pianist such as Thelonious Monk, as Cecil Taylor has pointed out, can do things that even the best classical pianists cannot: "That's where the validity of Monk's music is, in his technique."[9] But according to Western criteria, Monk has "no technique," or poor technical facility. His technique is valid only insofar as it helps him achieve his aims: his technique grows out of his musical conception. The young white musician, who had either learned how to read music and play his instrument through formal education or had learned improvisation, like the members of the Austin High gang, through imitation of black music, did not have the social or perceptual background of the black musician; thus white jazz rarely "feels" black. Therefore, whites, although they have often extended the dimensions of jazz music, have rarely altered its direction. Because a jazz musician cannot escape his own cultural referents and because the idioms of jazz force the musician to stand naked, emotionally, before his audience, jazz music has always maintained, indeed, has stimulated, a race consciousness.

Racial categories were further maintained and imposed by the economics of the recording industry. From the outset, recording companies developed separate "popular record" and "race record" lines. The former were available in white communities, the latter in black ghettos. Further, it made a great deal of difference to the musician, in terms of money and status, which label one recorded for. Paul Whiteman, the most vociferous white band leader employing black music (to some small extent) but not black musicians, became known to the white world as the "King of Jazz." By 1922, Whiteman was grossing over a million dollars a year. Black musicians, although they often made a superior living compared to other blacks or to anything they had previously received, did not begin to approach this kind of earning power. In fact, to earn a living, black musicians often had to record under dozens of different pseudonyms, for several different record companies, in order to evade contractual rules and agreements. Record companies developed "stables" of black artists who were occasionally recognized by jazz aficionados but were rarely given personal credit by the company and almost never received royalty fees for their work. The *race* and *popular* labels also tended to establish mutually exclusive audiences. A former owner of a black record store remembers the early twenties: "Colored people would form a line twice around the block when the latest record of Bessie or Ma or Clara [black blues singers] come

in . . . sometimes these records was bootlegged . . . for
four or five dollars apiece . . . nobody never asked for
Paul Whiteman; I doubt it they ever knew about him"[10]
The recording industry maintained racial discrimination of
the subtle separate-but-unequal variety. Whiteman received
the credit, the money, and the publicity for a music essentially not his own. Still more difficult for black musicians
to bear was Whiteman's stated aim: to show the "advance
which had been made in popular music from the day of
discordant early jazz to the melodious form of the present."[11]
This meant, in effect, that he was presenting an appropriated
music in heavily diluted form and was successfully selling it
as the real thing. This too has been a permanent aspect of
the recording business. During the twenties it was more or
less accepted. However, as early as 1935, even white music
critics like Panassie subjected this policy to severe criticism.

This kind of inherent racism was accepted without great
comment during the twenties partly because of the black
musician's desire to gain a degree of respectability within the
white world, one facet of the assimilative trend of the decade.
Fletcher Henderson, for example, one of the most original
and prolific of the black band leaders, openly embraced the
rather dehumanizing title of "Negro King of Jazz." He accepted the inherent *distinction* of being a Negro because it
implied acceptance, however token, within the white world.
As Cleaver has noted, ". . . prefixing anything with 'Negro'
automatically consigned it to an inferior category."[12] In fact,
Henderson's work did not become well known in the white
community until his collaboration with Benny Goodman, the
white "King of Swing," during the thirties. By the sixties,
this desire for white respectability had either been totally
spent or had become inverted into extreme antiwhite sentiment, and black musician Charles Mingus, for example, was
furious at even being addressed as a "jazz musician." He
stated that "to me the word jazz means nigger, discrimina-

tion, second-class citizenship, the whole back-of-the-bus bit."[13] However, the twenties, because it was a period of high expectation for the black culture, found the black musician going to great lengths to become a salable property. Perhaps this was why he often wore a foolish grin. Louis Armstrong was only one of the good black musicians who was known to record inferior material for the sake of gaining a wider (whiter) audience. Armstrong even introduced comic routines into his nightclub act as a ploy to increase the interest in his music: "Sometimes Zutty [his drummer] and I would do a specialty number together," he recalls. "Zutty, he's funny anyway, would dress up as one of those real loud and rough gals, with a short skirt, and a pillow in back of him. I was dressed in old rags, the beak of my cap turned around, like a tough guy, and he, or she [Zutty] was my gal."[14]

It is apparent that Armstrong was not ashamed of this kind of prostitution of his musical ability. The essential point to be grasped is that the black musician, and the Negro in general, did not see himself as other than *gaining* on the white culture. He had fought in the War to end all wars and was sharing in the general postwar affluence, and perhaps he didn't mind acting a little foolish as long as it was in the name of progress. Racism during this period, usually the case during prosperity and spreading affluence, *appeared* to be on the wane, and black and white America appeared to enjoy the tacit acceptance of each other. The word *appeared* is underscored because racism was there but not overtly on the mind of the black musician. It can be suggested then that, in Oppenheimer's phrase, "it is rarely deprivation as such which accounts for strain. . . . Rather, the deprivation must first be perceived by a group, and this can only be done if the group can compare itself with some other relevant group."[15] Black America during the twenties could not accurately compare itself with white America because it basically did not *perceive* itself to be separate from white America; that is, it did not consider itself to be outside the realm of mainstream American culture. Garvey failed precisely for this reason: his followers considered themselves essentially part of a greater America and thus could not accept emigration seriously, at least not as long as "things were getting better." Mingus's comments, however, suggest a black American who both accepts America as home and at the same time perceives it to be inherently alien territory. Black America, over the forty-odd years since the Depression, has become conscious of itself in relation to white America, and perhaps it was only through the exposure to and experience with white culture during the twenties that this black "self-consciousness" could come about at all. The twenties was, in terms of race relations, a kind of peak (or trough) in the cultural history of America. Today, racial progress is judged by the amount and kind of legislation that is being enforced; during the twenties it appeared that perhaps extreme legislation might not be necessary or, at least, that it could evolve *naturally* of its own accord and in its own time. The sense of urgency, of need for external pressure to hasten racial harmony seems to be a very modern phenomenon. Hence, in the North especially, there was also little overt hostility from the whites, no frantic *backlash* opposition to the integrationist tendencies of the twenties.

This decade was America's first experience with racial development in urban, industrial society. One universally recognized result of modern industrial society is what has been called the "fragmentation" of social groups into individuals. This was reflected in the *star* systems of the entertainment industry, like that of the movie world that catered to the prototypically "American" self-image, the sensibility of the average white American. This reduction of the social focus of the entertainment industry to the lowest common denominator of American society was not complete until the escapist films of the thirties. The Negro, however, was never catered to by any of the mass media, save the recording industry. Thus the examination of the "fragmentative" effects of urban society on the recorded black music of the decade gives us one of the few clues as to the nature of the new black self-image. The recording industry, for example, had created a substantial black *star* system with the Classic blues singers, notably females such as Bessie Smith and Ma Rainey, taking the place that white film stars held in white communities. These singers were gaining a kind of cultural permanence through recording, not unlike that created by films, which caused the black community to project group attributes on to specific individuals. Black musicians, therefore, gained a substantial amount of prestige if and when they recorded under their own names or when they were featured as "back up" men for the Classic blues singers. The soloist emerged from the group context through the *star* system. Yet the way in which the soloist remained integrated with the group as a whole indicates the manner in which black culture, as a whole, remained somewhat coherent throughout the "fragmentative" process. A prime example would be the Louis Armstrong "Hot Five" recordings of 1926. The "Hot Five" band was strictly a recording outfit and had rarely played together as a group outside of the recording studio. Armstrong's dominant influence was obvious. Hodeir has said of these records, in comparison to Armstrong's earlier work with Oliver, "With King Oliver, you listen to the *band,* here, you listen to Louis."[16] This was partially because Armstrong was positioned closer to the microphone in these later recordings. It was also a result of new musical developments of the twenties. The increased use of Western harmony caused the soloist to contrast his work with the chords being laid down by the rhythm section. Mellers has suggested that "only when harmonic solidarity was so clearly defined that it could exert its influence unconsciously could a true jazz polyphony be explored."[17] Armstrong was one of the first *compositional* improvisers; he spontaneously created melodic lines that sounded like preconceived melodic structures *in relation* to the harmonic and melodic direction of the rest of the band. Armstrong's sophistication in the advancement of what, in Western terms, would be considered basic contrapuntal technique was a function of his ability to sublimate—to "hear internally"—the formal rules of Western harmonic structure. Armstrong's achievement, then, was in his application of the techniques of the oral culture to solve problems previously approached only through Western methods. The Negro appeared in terms of Western standards to be naive, but it would be truer to say that he simply applied an intuitive approach to problems of structure. Jazz solos came to compose a running commentary on Western structures, such as the 32-bar song form, and this commentary was often ironic, or mocking, in tone. Armstrong himself was a master of the ironic use of Western song form, both as an instrumentalist and as a vocalist. The soloist's freedom became a function of his ability to extend or transcend the limitations of Western harmonic form through the application of an oral orientation. Thus, it can be suggested that the black culture avoided some of the alienating effects of urban, industrial society by remaining somewhat aloof, somewhat disassociated from the mainstream American culture, often at a subliminal level of operation but still evident in the *style* of black social patterns. Equally as important was the fact that they had maintained an alternative culture upon which to rely, one which was capable of solving some of the problems posed by urban, industrial society.

The integration of the individual into the society as a whole was also evident in the big band format of the twenties. In the large white bands, such as Whiteman's, the individual was generally submerged in the "section" work— i.e., the trumpet section, the saxophone section, or the rhythm section—and, in fact, these sections had section leaders, not unlike shop foremen in the factories, to integrate the small units into the whole organization. Occasionally a soloist, like the legendary Bix Beiderbecke, would rise out of this rigid structure for a few choruses, but, by and large, the large white bands did not attempt to integrate individual personalities into the group. The "melodious form" had very little to do with jazz tradition. The large Negro bands, however, attempted to maintain a "group feeling" that was a function of individual personalities. The better Negro arrangers evolved techniques that compensated for the large band format—Duke Ellington kept two separate "books" of arrangements, one for white audiences, one for blacks, and often went so far as to exchange parts in the middle of a piece ". . . because the man and the part weren't the same character"—or developed methods of presentation that transcended the restrictions to improvisation posed by the large organizations. Fletcher Henderson, for example, exploited the soloists as spontaneous voices by creating arrangements specifically for individual soloists. In brief, the large Negro bands, although they did in many cases require that the music be written—that the compositional process be somewhat formal—avoided the passivity of the white bands by employing oral techniques: the vocalized tone was present even in brass or reed "section" playing, the "blue tonality" of black music was found in almost all the written arrangements, and the rhythm became more complex, both in the rhythm section (piano, bass, drums, and guitar) and in the antiphonal arrangements. The introduction of the saxophone as a solo voice, which occurred primarily with the big bands, made the quality of vocalization more readily available to black instrumentalists, as that horn sounds like the human voice throughout its registers. In effect, black jazz soloists became more "human" sounding even though their context (the big band) was often more mechanized. Saxophonist Sidney Bechet, whose recordings of the late twenties contrasted the hard edge of Armstrong's recordings with a melancholy that recalled the intense "mood" of some of

Ellington's work, played the instrument with a sensual passion and employed a distinctly "singing" tone. By the thirties, the saxophone had begun to challenge the trumpet for the dominant position in jazz improvisation. Thus, the drive for a "human" sound appeared to be all the more imperative to the oral culture in the mechanized context. Although there was a tendency in the big band format itself to diminish the importance of individual expression, the best of these bands, and the best of the big band arrangers, such as Don Redman, created a big city context for the basics of oral tradition.

The optimism of the twenties was well on the wane by the time the stock market collapsed in 1929. The white jazz musician had become a new kind of white American, one who, in effect, no longer represented the sentiments of white America as a whole once the initial interest in black culture had been spent. Also, the large Negro bands that played before white audiences found that commercialism had infected the process of creativity and emotional release. As Don Redman has said, "We did a lot of traveling on the road and were almost always playing for white dances . . . [we] were considered a very commercial property then. We had a terrific band but I wasn't able to do the kind of jazz things I might have in the places we were playing."[18] Even white jazzmen felt the pressure of commercialization. Benny Goodman has noted that "when we started the band, the only purpose we had was to play music . . . and the rest [the other musicians], they had a purpose. It was their life, it was important to them. . . . But something happens when you find out that what you're doing is no longer music—that it's become entertainment. It's a subtle thing and affects what you're playing. Your whole attitude changes."[19] I suggest that the mass conformity of urban, industrial society was a primary cause of the disaffection of urban blacks. The "entertainment" aspect of which Benny Goodman speaks is, in fact, part of the American process that forces communication through media (whether mass media such as films or the

more immediate communication processes such as live music)
to conform to the taste of the lowest common denominator.
Within the black culture, the lowest common denominator
had traditionally been involved in the creative process of
musical invention; within white culture, the average man
had had no experience whatsoever in emotional expression
through nonverbal modes of communication. "Entertainment" in the hands of Bessie Smith or Louis Armstrong
became a kind of high Art and often served as a cathartic
group ritual for the black masses. This is, in part, the function of music in the black community because of its foundations in an oral tradition. Whereas white society in America
tends to be *conformist,* black culture is collective, or communal. This is due, partially, to its reliance on music as a
socializing agent. Black culture did not need *formal* entertainment the way that whites did. Rather, it sought an outlet
through which Negroes could more or less entertain themselves. The commercial orientation of whites during the
twenties was primarily responsible for the subsequent return
to segregated (i.e., black jazz for black audiences) music of
the thirties and was a major event in the evolution of a self-
consciousness within the black culture.

The great enthusiasm for the emotional honesty of black
music appeared, by the end of the twenties, to have been
absorbed by the fad consciousness of the decade, indicating
that white America's emotional needs are in some way predicated upon and, at times, overridden by a less than "hu-
manistic" group orientation. The theory of "planned obsolescence" that is at the heart of the American commercial
structure seems also to be applicable to the shift of black
music in white America back and forth between the categories of *emotional need* and *social fashion.* White America's
threshold for black music as fulfilling an emotional need
appears to be in constant flux (it must go out of fashion in
order to come back into fashion), responding to the materially

oriented principle of "planned obsolescence," as applied to more purely psychological functions. In short, the white need for black music is not only closely associated with prosperity in white America, but is also a function of white America's fashion consciousness, i.e., how white America *sees* black culture at the time and the role in which black musicians are cast. The heightened romanticism in the music of some black musicians during the late twenties, such as that of Webster, Ellington, and Bechet, seemed to bespeak both a nostalgia for the pre-urban, nonwhite oriented condition of jazz playing and a rejection of the more raucous music which white America had so glibly accepted as essentially "Negroid."

The cultural optimism and assimilative trend of the "Jazz Age" were doomed to failure because of the ambiguities upon which they were built. On the one hand, the white culture had miscalculated the depths of black spirituality by fastening on the "hedonistic" interpretation of black culture. This misconception contributed to the peculiarly American character of black culture and to its solidarity, if only because it provided a point of view against which black Americans reacted or to which they made accommodations. The more basic disaffection of black America, however, was present, in a strength, from the onset of the decade. One symptom of this was the wide appeal of Garvey's back-to-Africa movement; the black musician's drive to create an "ethnically singular" voice was another, more subtle and perhaps more pervasive. It therefore seems reasonable to assert that the traditional view of the "Jazz Age," in not taking into account the basic orientations of Western culture as opposed to those of a black American oral culture, has missed an underlying source of strain within urban America and that contemporary racial misunderstandings, as they too are based on interpretations of urban societies, have their roots in these misconceptions of the twenties.

4

The Evolution
of the Black Underground:
1930–1947

There is a great deal of literature available on American jazz of the thirties, most of it concerned with white musicians, white audiences ("jitterbugs"), and white music. The accepted view of the jazz of this period, one which is still maintained by many jazz critics, is that the "swing era" found increasingly integrated bands—the Goodman big band and the small "band within the band" that featured Negroes Teddy Wilson and Lionel Hampton are cited as highlights—and that these integrated bands continued to "refine" black music. This view can be confirmed in the jazz "polls" that began in the middle thirties wherein no Negro players won top positions, few Negroes even made the listings, and Harry James invariably won top trumpet over Louis Armstrong.[1] These same critics generally viewed the radical black jazz that surfaced in New York around 1914 as a break in the jazz continuum and often contend that the angry "bebop" musicians were a phenomenon unique to New York City, springing full-blown on the jazz scene after a handful of informal sessions at Minton's. I intend here to point out that the seeds of a black "underground" music were present in the thirties and, through a brief musical and cultural analysis, to trace the origins of the black "underground." The lack of

Photographer **Tom Copi** began photographing musicians in his home town of Ann Arbor, Michigan in 1965. His move to California in 1972 coincided with the opening of Keystone Korner as a jazz club, and Mr. Copi credits Keystone-owner Todd Barkan as his primary mentor in the field of jazz photography. His photos have graced the covers of countless jazz magazines and record albums and appeared in publications throughout the world.

MILES DAVIS at ease with his trumpet during a two-day festival in Newport, Rhode Island in September 1975. Photo © by Tom Copi/San Francisco.

ORNETTE COLEMAN shook up the jazz community in 1959 when he arrived in New York from the West Coast with his angular compositions and highly-vocalized saxophone style. But by 1978 he was featured here at the White House Jazz Festival in Washington, D.C. During the 1970s he has recorded only sporadically and made few public appearances, citing the politics of the music business as the reason for his self-imposed exile. Photo © by Tom Copi/San Francisco.

COUNT BASIE explains one of the finer points of an arrangement to his band during the 1977 Monterey Jazz Festival. Seen at far left is veteran guitarist Freddie Green. Photo by Tom Copi/San Francisco.

LOUIS "POPS" ARM-STRONG, the musical revolutionary as grand old man, singing, mugging, and having a ball while he educates another generation of students at Ann Arbor's Hill Auditorium, 1966. Photo © by Tom Copi /San Francisco.

RAHSAAN ROLAND KIRK, the multi-instrumentalist and tireless improviser, is shown during the 1969 Newport Jazz Festival. Photo © by Tom Copi/San Francisco.

EARL "FATHA" HINES performs at a 1978 benefit for San Francisco jazz radio station KJAZ. His pianistic innovations led to the freeing of the rhythm section, and thus to the bebop era. Photo © by Tom Copi/San Francisco.

BO DIDDLEY, who built his following through the repetition of one highly infectious rhythm pattern, caught on with the youth of the world well before he headlined at this 1969 Rock & Roll revival at Detroit's Cobo Arena. Photo © by Tom Copi/San Francisco.

CECIL TAYLOR (left), **RANDY WESTON** (center), and **McCOY TYNER,** all modern piano virtuosos, compare notes backstage during 1978. Their spiritual elder, Thelonious Monk, peers gleefully over Weston's shoulder from the wall of San Francisco's Keystone Korner. Photo © by Tom Copi/San Francisco.

DIZZY GILLESPIE, of the big cheeks, demonstrates his "incorrect" trumpet technique during a 1975 concert at San Francisco's Civic Auditorium. Photo © by Tom Copi/San Francisco.

ART BLAKEY, whose hard driving quintets provided an antidote to the "cool school" during the 1950s, continued during the 60s and 70s to serve as a veritable bebop university with a list of graduates that includes Freddie Hubbard, Wayne Shorter, Horace Silver, Donald Byrd, and Lee Morgan. The drummer is shown here at a 1976 performance at Carnegie Hall. Photo © by Tom Copi/San Francisco.

DUKE ELLINGTON captured during the 1967 Newport Jazz Festival, with alto experts Benny Carter (left) and Johnny Hodges sharing thoughts in the background. Photo © by Tom Copi/San Francisco.

JAMES BROWN, "the hardest working man in show business," on stage at the 1969 Newport Jazz Festival. By the late 1960s traditional jazz events had broadened their scope to include "soul" performers. Photo © by Tom Copi/San Francisco.

ULIAN "CANNONBALL" ADDERLEY (left) and brother **NAT ADDERLEY** led ome of the most commercially successful quintets of the 1960s (their hit records included "Dis Here" and "Mercy, Mercy, Mercy"), photographed at the 1975 Berkeley Jazz Festi-al just prior to Cannonball's death. Photo © by Tom Copi/San Francisco.

CHARLES MINGUS, an important figure in the transition from the intellectualism of post-war bebop to the emotionalism of 1960s "free" jazz, is seen here at the 1976 Berkeley Jazz Festival. His death in 1979 was felt throughout the worlds of jazz and rock music—both categories he rejected. Photo © by Tom Copi/San Francisco.

HORACE SILVER, seen here at The Keystone Korner in 1978, had a hit record with Art Blakey and the Jazz Messengers as far back as 1955, but his highly physical approach to the piano had a profound effect on such modernists as Cecil Taylor as well. For years he has epitomized the "soul school" of jazz piano. Photo © by Tom Copi/San Francisco.

ELVIN JONES, whose tumbling triplet feeling on drums recalled the sanctified freedom of gospel music while it fed the fire behind John Coltrane's legendary quartet, leads his own group at a California concert. Photo © by Tom Copi/San Francisco.

RAY CHARLES, the "high priest himself," during a 1977 San Francisco club date. His amalgam of gospel, blues and jazz opened up a vast new radio audience for black music during the 50s and 60s. Photo © by Tom Copi/San Francisco.

PHILLY JOE JONES, the quintessential bebop drummer by virtue of his performances, live and on record, with virtually every major innovator of the idiom, is shown here with the Bill Evans trio during 1978. Photo © by Tom Copi/San Francisco.

JIMI HENDRIX playing at The Fifth Dimension, a Detroit teen club, in 1967. Hendrix went to England, gained international recognition, then returned to America where he influenced popular music throughout the world. Photo © by Tom Copi/San Francisco.

(Left to Right) **B.B. KING, MISSISSIPPI FRED McDOWELL, WILLIE MAE "BIG MAMA" THORNTON** (w/cup), **JUNIOR WELLS, ROOSEVELT SYKES** (seated), captured in a rare photo backstage at the first annual Ann Arbor Jazz Festival, 1969. Promoted by a core of radical college students, the festival was part of a greater extra-curricular effort centered on the anti-war movement. Photo © by Tom Copi/San Francisco.

THE PERSUASIONS, the ultimate street corner singing group, whose unadorned four part harmony recalls the church and foreshadowed avant-garde groups like The World Saxophone Quartet. Photo © by Tom Copi/San Francisco.

DON CHERRY and **ANGELA DAVIS** backstage at The Keystone Korner following Cherry's appearance there with the Old and New Dreams band, 1978. Photo © by Tom Copi/San Francisco.

BETTY CARTER at Carnegie Hall for the Newport Jazz Festival, 1978. Known for her "instrumental" style of jazz singing, she was also in the fore-front of the jazz musician's struggle for economic independence, starting her own record company during the 1970s. Photo © by Tom Copi/San Francisco.

ANTHONY BRAXTON, who often performs by himself in clubs and concerts throughout Europe and the U.S., is shown here amid his forest of saxophones at the Keystone Korner, 1977. His highly intellectual compositions often sport titles that resemble mathematical formulas. Photo © by Tom Copi/San Francisco.

L JARREAU emerged in the late 1970s one of the most prominent new jazz gers. His ability to reproduce vocally the und of the drums, horns, and guitars re-lls the African synthesis of all instruments the human voice. Photo © by Tom Copi/ n Francisco.

CHUCK BERRY, legendary father of rock and roll, plays at a Detroit teen club, 1969. After great success in the 1950s, his fame increased in the 1960s and '70s after acknowledgments from many white rockers, including The Beatles and Rolling Stones. Photo © by Tom Copi/San Francisco.

DEXTER GORDON, one of the few first-generation be-bop horn players from the 1940s to remain active into the 1980s, caught in a typically pensive mood during a 1975 appearance. Photo © by Tom Copi/San Francisco.

EUBIE BLAKE, the ragtime piano professor, sings his classics for an audience at San Francisco's Zellerbach Auditorium in 1976. Known to millions of Americans because of his frequent television appearances, Blake likes to talk about the days when the piano was part of the bordello rather than the night club. Photo © by Tom Copi/San Francisco.

ARETHA FRANKLIN earned the title "first lady of soul" by delivering to the popular song the spiritual intensity she learned with her father's gospel choir. Here she lays it on the line during a 1977 performance in Oakland. Photo © by Tom Copi/San Francisco.

THE ART ENSEMBLE OF CHICAGO uses theatrics and non-Western instrumentation for individual and collective improvisations. Photo © by Tom Copi/San Francisco.

JON HENDRICKS, author and star of "The Evolution of the Blues," a musical revue of the history of Black music in America, seen in a 1977 production. Hendricks is a master of "vocalese"—the art of putting words to classic bebop horn solos. Photo © by Tom Copi/San Francisco.

FREDDIE HUBBARD at the Berkeley Ja Festival in 1978 demonstrates the Mil Davis dictum: "You can tell the way I pl by the way I stand." Photo © by Tom Co /San Francisco.

literature concerning black music during the thirties is understandable since black culture is basically not a literate culture; in fact, the absence of literary information is itself a kind of proof of both the oral roots of black music and its "underground" status.

By labeling the black music of this period *underground* communication, I am trying to establish that black musicians, after their initial exposure to Western forms and white society during the twenties, gradually became self-conscious of developing a separate and "ethnically singular" idiom and that this was possible only in light of their prior exposure to, and partial acceptance by, a wider American audience. It would not be true to say that black musicians developed a particularly "political" consciousness during this period, although British historian Eric Hobsbaum has hinted at an association of black musicians of this period with the Communist movement in America.[2] The nature of the "underground" was cultural rather than political, a "communications revolution" that preceded the political revolution. It was the cultural *exclusivity,* the self-conscious separation from mainstream America of black music and black culture that gives leverage to the notion of a black underground and to the conception of the underground as a potential base for social action. Just as a "voting bloc" has weight insomuch as it is able, by its very nature, to exclude the participation of others, so too a "cultural bloc" gains strength from its exclusive nature. The strength of both the bebop and rhythm-and-blues idioms that developed out of the black music of the thirties was that they excluded from participation many Americans (most of them were white, although many were of the black middle-class) who, as a matter of *taste* and of cultural *stance,* were unable to identify with the new assertion of "blackness." Since the survival of the bebop and rhythm-and-blues idioms parallels the survival of a style of social organization, the overt ideologies of black musicians, whether they were influenced by Communism or the Black Muslims, are perhaps less important than the social nature of black music itself.

It could be said with a certain amount of accuracy that the oral culture was, by nature, an underground culture in the context of literate America; that simply being a Negro in America was grounds for nonconformity. Each member of the oral culture was, in terms of the criteria of the literate culture, a "deviant," engaging in behavior that reevaluated as it was during the "Jazz Age" was nonetheless contrary to the accepted norm. However, the consolidation of black culture during the thirties, although due in large part to this basic opposition of orality and literacy, was brought on by external pressure as well. One issue was central to the notion of a black underground: to what extent was the oral culture driven underground, i.e., to what extent was its cohesion forced upon it, and to what extent was it naturally underground in terms of white America? These two questions are part of a single, larger question of the relationship of the black man to white America and compose, in effect, a single inquiry: any assertion from the black culture will invite a kind of cultural retribution from white America with the result that black activity is never purely an assertion. Conversely, strong pressures from the side of white America will cause a subsequent regrouping around the principles of the oral tradition within black America, so that no assertion of "blackness" is ever without its counterpart on the side of white America.

It is self-evident that internal cohesiveness can be the result of external pressure. In Robert Ardrey's formula, *amity*, or internal cohesion, is in some sense "equal to the sum of the forces of enmity and hazard" arrayed against a given culture, *enmity* being defined as "those forces of antagonism and hostility originating in members of one's own species."[3] Already the victims of last-hired, first-fired policies prior to the Depression, American Negroes fared much worse during the Depression than whites did. The criteria for job qualification were thrown back on racial categories. This was particularly true in the entertainment industry where, for example, radio stations refused to hire Negroes for session work, and the Musicians' Union, segregated for all practical purposes during the thirties, did not arbitrate in favor of black musicians. The "race" recording field, too, suffered a great deal during the Depression and was the first line dropped from major record labels as hard times got harder. This reduced the studio work for black musicians to an all-time low. Even touring bands played on increasingly segregated circuits, like the Theatre Owners and Bookers Association that became the major outlet for Negro "acts."[4] This kind of imposition of racial discrimination contributed to the consolidation of the music industry into black and white camps.

Just as in the late nineteenth century when Creole musicians in New Orleans had been forced to "go Uptown" or quit the music profession, racial discrimination during the Depression actually had the effect of strengthening the lower-class Negro culture by defining it as the sole territory for black expression. Those Negroes who refused to accept this definition were forced out of the music business. Sidney Bechet, for example, opened up a shoe-shine parlor. Many black musicians returned to the lower-class black culture with the attitude that "my enemy's enemy is my friend," but it was all much more complicated and subtle than this. The concept of "secondary deviance," for example, includes the notion that if a person fails to be accepted in one role, he may gravitate toward an alternative role of an opposite character.[5] The "secondary deviant" seeking a role of "opposite" character from that normally offered by white society can find no better models than those provided by lower-class black culture where even the tenets of the dominant "work ethic" appear to have been abandoned. The black musician who had been rejected, seemingly overnight, by the white entertainment establishment turned his rejection into a positive stance by more closely embracing the role of musician in an exclusively black environment. Thus, exclusively black music, all the more attractive now to those musicians who had been rebuffed by white society, provided an opportunity for them to turn their rejection into an assertion of identity. Proof of this appears everywhere in the music of the period. The "white" jazz became more formalized, more precision-orientated (more Western in general), and the "black" jazz became once again improvisational, casual, and heavily blues orientated.

One sign of growing racial solidarity in the black lower-class was the birth of the Black Muslim movement in 1930. The major argument of W. D. Fard, its founder, was that the white man and Christianity were evil and that his, Fard's, teaching would destroy the white devil. The Muslim movement used religious allegory to build a foundation of black *mystique* that incorporated the denial of Western culture. Many black musicians became active Muslims as early as the thirties, but for the most part these men—who by the forties had taken to stopping band rehearsals to bow toward Mecca —were more actively escaping the problem of racial discrimination than confronting it. As Dizzy Gillespie has said of these early Muslims, "They been hurt and they're trying to get away from it."[6] However, racial in-grouping in the music business was not built simply on a foundation of a black *mystique*. It became clear after the assimilation process of the twenties that there were certain effects that could be achieved only through the application of oral techniques and that these techniques themselves could be developed only through extended exposure to lower-class black culture. So, if you lived "white," you played "white"; if you lived "black," you played "black." Miles Davis recently said,

". . . you got to have them brothers there because there are things that they do that they did when they were kids that the white boy don't know about."[7] Davis attributes the reasons for the way an individual plays—and, in fact, musical approach in general—to environment.

Every period in the evolution of black music has a locality that seems to spawn for years to come the new style, or *approach,* of black musicians. During the thirties, the Southwest in general and Kansas City in particular became such an area. There are many reasons why the seeds of a black underground should have taken root there. The primary one was that this part of the country, unlike the cities of the urban North, was both geographically and sociologically close to the origins of black oral tradition. While the rest of the country had been moving swiftly toward a more commercial jazz music, this section of America had remained the blues capital of the world. Blues of the rural, or pre-urban, type never lost its appeal, and solo blues singers remained big favorites. Interestingly enough, a high proportion of these rural blues singers were blind. It can be assumed that blind Negroes had little enough opportunity for employment, especially during the Depression, and therefore became musicians by default, but this glosses over an important aspect: blindness is potentially an advantage when dealing in so heavily an oral/aural occupation as blues singing. Blind blues singers, from Blind Lemon Jefferson through Ray Charles, have wielded a certain amount of authority within the blues idiom. This authority comes from an obvious *personal* commitment to blues techniques; the vocalized tone is heightened and the intensely individualized presentation of the song is strengthened, for blindness is itself an agent of isolation. Just as important is the authority the black community grants to blind singers, as if blindness were both an exaggeration of "the black man's burden" and a physical metaphor for black life in America. Neither of these explanations adequately covers the importance of the blind blues singer as a dominant image in the psyche of the black culture because his importance is so closely involved with the concept of orality, itself so much a part of black life.

As blues became more the voice and idiom of an underground America, the whites who were attracted to it were no longer the kind of intellectuals who had loved Chicago jazz for its hedonism, but were themselves, for the most part, victims of social oppression. The rural bluesmen were "discovered" by the white culture when, during the Depression, men such as Alan Lomax went through the South and West recording their music, and when others, like Woody Guthrie, became involved in their music as natural vehicles for the expression of more generalized songs of oppression. The great Labor movement of the Depression gave birth to Guthrie's type of music and to occasionally remarkable interracial organizations such as the Southern Tenant Farmers' Union. It became the fountainhead for a new American "folk" tradition, one of overt social protest. Perhaps the main distinction between this folk tradition and the original blues idiom, aside from the fact that the folk tradition lacked any *oral* technique, was that the protest songs of the Labor movement were organized around specific social ills, while the blues was concerned either with personal problems or with grievous human failings. The same distinction can be drawn between classical Marxism and the rhetoric of Malcolm X.

Kansas City was a kind of cultural halfway house, steeped in the rural culture but growing all the time as an urban center, and the musical idioms that evolved there were often hybrid. Two new blues strains developed in the thirties there, one characterized by "shouting" singers and the other by sophisticated instrumentalists. In the early part of the decade, these idioms were both part of a single form of black expression. The "shouting" singers worked with eight- or nine-piece bands and toured throughout the area, playing and singing blues (almost to the exclusion of other idioms) to exclusively black audiences. The very size of these bands reflected the urban influence, where large bands were the fashion, although outside of Kansas City itself, the audience was only marginally "urban" in character. Their blues was loosely arranged, although not written down, and built on "riffs," or unwritten phrases played in unison or in "barber-shop" harmony, behind the singer. The saxophone became the mainstay of these units because the vocalized tone imitated so well the shouting style of the singer. The sophistication of the urban atmosphere showed up in the phrasing of "shouters" like Jimmy Rushing and Joe Turner who developed styles of singing that were rhythmically advanced from the older, rural blues styles. They would place their lyrics either behind or in front of the beat, rather than "on the beat," creating the kind of anticipation generated by black preachers but in secularized context now. Although this urban "shouting" style was closely linked to black Christianity—one contemporary blues singer told me that "Spirituals are the same thing as the blues, only you're usin' 'Jesus' instead of 'baby,' "—it was, as black Christianity often was itself, non-Western in orientation. Jones has suggested that the "honking" saxophone players who worked with the "shouting" singers were consciously playing as non-Western as possible as a reaction against "the softness and 'legitimacy' which had crept into black instrumental music with the advent of swing."[8] The radio had been bringing the white swing music into the South for several years by this time, and it is possible that the Kansas City bluesmen were consciously creating a style that was a reaction against this white approach. On the other hand, because it is difficult to separate the function of music in black culture from its form, it can be suggested that the music was becoming more non-Western because there was a need for an outlet for more primary black social aggression. This idea fits well with the notion of a black underground; i.e., music as a *cultural voice*. The audience was as much a part of the musical presentation as the performer, and the shouting blues singer, in time, became part of a highly stylized ritual wherein his emotional excesses (his screaming and pacing which the audience loved) could be easily faked, for the purpose of creating a group catharsis. The singer would, at the appropriate moment, fall to his knees and cajole the audience; the horn player would likewise hit the floor and play as "unmusical" (in Western terms) as possible, usually doing the singer one better. Perhaps the primary reason for the divergence of this blues tradition from the jazz tradition was that these men wanted to perform effectively and were perhaps only incidentally concerned with musical innovation. Therefore, they would play into the emotional hands of whatever crowd had gathered. As Louis Jordan, one of the "honking" tenor players, has said of the jazz players, "Those guys . . . really wanted to play mostly for themselves, and I still wanted to play for the people."[9]

Thus, during the thirties, a rift opened in the lower-class black community as the more sophisticated members—those who had become "world-wise" during the urban secularization process—gravitated to the jazz idioms and the more *country* members congregated around the rhythm-and-blues. The jazz player had traditionally been in the social vanguard of the black lower-class, and this rift only served to reinforce his leadership in the urban, as opposed to rural, sectors of that community. Again, it should be noted that during the early thirties the rhythm-and-blues and the jazz strains were not two distinct spheres of activity and that only with further urbanization did the divergence, both in the presentation of the music and in the intentions of the musicians, become noticeable. It was true, however, that the jazz players, who had either been apprenticed to all-Negro circus bands or had, at least, been exposed to the highly commercialized "swing" formula, were becoming in-group oriented. Perhaps the strongest motivation for the development of a "musician's jazz," as opposed to a "people's jazz," was musical consideration, although, as mentioned, it is difficult to separate the form of black music from its social function. However, as one critic recently said, "The increasing popularity of swing arrangements on the Henderson model led to a general similarity of style in all the big bands, Negro and white. Goodman, Shaw, the Dorseys, Barnet, Hines, Calloway, Teddy Hill, Webb, were all approaching the same standards of proficiency. There is a terrifying record, an anthology called *The Great Swing Bands* on which most of these bands are represented. If they are played without consulting notes or labels, *it is impossible to distinguish one from the other*."[10] The drive for an ethnically singular voice and the demand within the oral culture for individuality above all else—heightened by the conformity of urban society—dictated that a new kind of jazz be evolved. The new style evolved away from large audiences partly because those audiences were responsible for the watering down of musical content.

Equally as important was the "status disparity" black musicians met while on the road with big bands. Roy Eldridge, who joined Artie Shaw's white band during this period, said, ". . . one thing you can be sure of, as long as I'm in America, I'll never in my life work with a white band again! Man, when you're on the stage, you're great, but as soon as you come off, you're nothing. It's not worth the glory, not worth the money, not worth anything."[11] Even the all-Negro bands that played for large white audiences during the thirties felt this kind of status disparity. Eldridge was one of the better-known black players of the era, so it can be assumed that many black musicians underwent much worse treatment offstage than did the more famous black "personalities." Status disparity—which was "great" while on stage (the Negro in his *place*) and "nothing" offstage—contributed to the peer-group orientation of the new black jazz.

Perhaps the most important aspect of Kansas City jazz was what has been called the "joy of playing" that abounded in that city. The institution of the "jam session" originated about this time. These sessions would take place informally, on a working musician's off-hours, and the emotional release involved was in direct proportion to the status disparity experienced while on the job. Often these sessions would last for days, literally, and soloists would extend their improvisation—so abruptly curtailed by the big-band format and by the time limit of recordings—for dozens of choruses, attempting to "cut" (i.e., to show up) the other musicians. This spirit of friendly, even intimate, competition, not unlike that of the New Orleans period, was partially a reaction to the economic orientation of the white entertainment industry, wherein a musician's worth was equated with the salary he could command or the number of high-status jobs he was offered. One such jam session was described by Sam Price: "I remember once at the Subway Club on Eighteenth Street, I came by a session at about ten o'clock and then went home to clean up and change my clothes. I came back a little after one o'clock and they were still playing the same tune."[12] Clearly, only the most dedicated jazz fans, those firmly rooted in the oral tradition of extended improvisation (i.e., the musicians themselves), could sustain an interest in this kind of playing. As jazz playing broke out of the restrictions imposed by the swing formulas, albeit at first informally, the notion of music being work rather than play seemed to fall by the wayside. This provided a basis for the black musician to establish himself, once more, as one individual who was saying and doing what he pleased—outside the pale of white economics—and getting the support of his peer group. The fact that white society was bidding for his services only enhanced his self-imposed isolation.

The economics of Kansas City nightlife encouraged this stance. The city was kept prosperous even during the Depression by a crime syndicate known as the Pendergast machine. As the rest of the country became steeped in the conservatism of poverty and escapism *toward* middle-class vacuity (as opposed to the escapism of the twenties that was decidedly *away from* middle-class norms) through such commercialized modes as the Busby Berkeley *Gold Diggers* films or the music (often called "jazz") of Guy Lombardo and Wayne King, Kansas City people were enjoying a nightlife that rivaled the legendary heydays of both Chicago and New Orleans. In relation to the importance of Kansas City as the birthplace of the radical, underground music of the forties, this nightlife cannot be minimized, for it was anything but coincidental to innovation in black music. Just as poverty encourages in those of middle-class aspiration even stricter enforcement of Puritan codes and emotional repression, it encouraged an attitude of "if you ain't got nothing, you got nothing to lose" in those non-Puritan in their orientation. This attitude was manifest in the Kansas City sessions. The easy money offered by the fast nightlife further encouraged both social and musical experimentation. The "joy of playing" in Kansas City was close in spirit to the joy of being free from the Western restrictions and inhibitions; indeed, the nightlife of black musicians can be seen as a physical manifestation of their distance from the daylife work ethic of mainstream America.

The social clichés surrounding the jazz musician during the twenties were gradually being replaced. As competition was no longer based on economics, but rather upon musical conception and execution, the music itself became the most important increment of prestige among black players. This music made conscious departures from the swing music; it once again cultivated the accidental and spontaneous over the control and precision that had come to characterize white swing. The white aesthetic was summed up by Benny Goodman: "I am such a bug on accuracy in performance, about playing in tune, and want just the proper note values . . . in the written parts, I wanted it to sound as exact as the band could possibly make it."[13] Conversely, black musicians, even within the big band context, developed idioms that relied on no written parts. Count Basie's band had up to seventeen men playing harmonically and rhythmically advanced music without any written music. The black player, even as he was becoming more involved with harmonic exploration, relied on his ear rather than his ability to read music to find his way through the technical maze. In the midst of an increasingly complex environment, the black musician turned to the free-flowing oral modes; hence, he played "off the beat" to avoid the stagnant feel of Goodman's "on the beat" precision; he used increased vocalization, or tone "impurity," to help break through the passive detachment of big band work and to return the emotional honesty to jazz idioms. And, above all else, he played the blues.

If one accepts Leadbelly's definition of the blues as "a feeling" rather than as a specific harmonic form, it is an easy matter to relate the musical innovations of Kansas City to the oral tradition. This is not to suggest that the Kansas City musicians did not use the standard 12-bar form because of course they did, often to the exclusion of other forms. But accepting the "feeling" definition allows one to interpret the music as part of a larger cultural movement and to make distinctions between the use of the blues *form*, which many whites were employing, and the development of new techniques of blues *feeling*. The innovations came out of the larger bands first and were expanded upon during the smaller jam sessions. Bands such as Bennie Moten's were crucial to the development of jazz because they proved that those innovations had a sound economic foundation and that the Negro's musical intuitions need not be sacrificed to commercial conformity so that the black musician could earn a living. The "musician's" music that was being played in the informal sessions was given professional credibility when it was assimilated into the working environment of the black musician and established new standards throughout the jazz world. One technique used by Moten's 1932 band was the old call and response pattern of the blues idiom. His arrangements were never written down and many of the section riffs (unison or harmony phrases spontaneously improvised by the horn section) and head riffs (melodic or lead instrument playing, also often improvised) were similar to those of the developing rhythm-and-blues units. Because Moten was a close friend of Pendergast and had more or less complete control of the jobs in Kansas City, the innovations of his band became virtually standard for the area. His basic achievement was freeing the rhythmic *feel* of big band blues playing, using a steady chording guitar instead of the more frantic banjo player, and encouraging the "walking" bass figures, wherein the bass player was free to interpret to some extent both the time feel and the harmonic structure.

When pianist Count Basie took over Moten's band in 1934, he freed the time feeling further by de-emphasizing the use of his left hand and playing hornlike piano "fills" with his right. His bass player, Walter Page, continued to extend the role of the "walking" bass—to be fully exploited later by Jimmy Blanton and Oscar Pettiford—while guitarist Freddie Green provided subtle but steady guitar comping. Page and Green handled a large part of the time-keeping chores, thus freeing drummer Jo Jones to explode occasional "bombs" with his foot pedal—accents that gave the improvisation an extra kick—and to employ his high-hat cymbal to "lean" on the off beats, creating a rhythmic feel more propulsive than anything developed by "on the beat" white swing bands.

Jones elevated the art of drumming to a plateau of complexity unheard of since the days of Congo Square and, along with Chick Webb, provided the basis for Kenny Clarke's style of drumming in the forties. Clarke, by transferring the time-keeping from the drums to the ride cymbal, fully liberated the drummer's left hand and feet to "imply" the time with myriad accents as if to recall the intricacy of "primitive" African drummers. Ultimately, by the sixties, drummers like Milford Graves and Beaver Harris had dispensed with formal time-keeping entirely. It is significant to note that particularly after the twenties, black music generally became simultaneously more "primitive" in terms of rhythmic feel and complexity as improvisation became more sophisticated harmonically. The most radical rhythmic innovations have served to reaffirm the most basic aspect of black music. Basie's rhythm section was a supreme example of group mutuality, of collectivity in the oral tradition, which Dickie Wells has likened to "nothing less than a Cadillac motor with the force of a Mack truck—they more or less gave you a *ride*, then a *push*.[14] The idea of the soloist "riding" on top of the rhythm section foreshadows the basis of the small bebop groups of the forties for which Basie's section certainly provided a working model.

Perhaps Basie's outstanding achievement was the way he "turned riffs from decoration into substance."[15] Unlike Ellington's complex arranging, which had the sound of the orchestra as a whole in mind, Basie employed the unwritten riff structure to encourage adventurous solo work. He used standard popular tunes and many 12-bar tunes to build tension through the riff structure upon which the soloist could launch his inventions. Basie's approach can be seen as an alternative method from Ellington's of integrating the individual into the group. His work encouraged individual exploration, the dominant premise behind the revolutionary music that followed. Thus, if Ellington was, as he has been called, the "father" of modern jazz, Basie was the midwife who delivered the blues safely into contemporary jazz idioms. Basie's genius soloist was Lester Young, whose playing became the major influence on almost all the younger saxophone players as well as on the great Billie Holiday's singing technique.[16] Young played "modern" and although his modernism seemed to come from his use of comparatively advanced harmonic knowledge, it probably came from his rhythmic conception out of which even his harmonic ideas flowed. His insistence on the rhythmic priorities of jazz created a bridge across the stagnating stream of swing which, in Ross Russell's phrase, had become "polluted" by the arrangers; this made possible the even more complex rhythmic development of the bop style.[17] Young owed much of his achievement to the solo room provided by Basie's riff/solo structure. Within this structure, the individual musician was actively *involved,* as were the supporting musicians who were now no longer left to the devices of an external arranger. This reaffirmation of spontaneous improvisation was, in fact, an advanced application of basic blues "technique," blues being defined as a "feeling."

In urban culture, the treatment accorded the blues idiom —the amount of reliance on oral techniques as well as the social role blues playing fulfills—is an indication of the extent to which the black community is overtly offering alternatives to mainstream values. The rhythm-and-blues idiom that had become so highly ritualized, yet still retained its vitality, was the popularized expression of this theory; the ritualization was a function of the need for a peculiarly black outlet of social activity, the "ethnically singular" voice expressed through group catharsis. The jazz idiom can be taken to represent a more highly intellectualized assault on white value structures, whether social, psychological, or aesthetic. This sophistication was perculiar to the urban environment inasmuch as black music was not a clear *reaction* against

Western values until such time as it came into direct *conflict* with those values in a public arena on a mass scale. Oral modes of communication advanced during the thirties through the new uses found for vocalization and rhythmic freedom in the music and, more generally, through the reintegration of the blues idiom into the urban environment. The traditional notion of the thirties as the "swing era," then, appears one-sided in light of the evidence of increasing cultural consolidation around the blues in Kansas City. Perhaps the extent of the disparity between traditional notions and cultural realities can best be gauged by the profound shock most music critics felt upon first hearing the bebop (or bop) style of jazz in the early forties.

This "radical" style of playing was years in the preparation. Its spiritual leader, Charles Parker, was a teen-aged boy growing up in Kansas City when the blues idiom reemerged as the dominant idiom of black expression, and so the Kansas City experience in general can be seen to be the major musical contribution to the new radicalism. Certainly Parker's use of blues techniques reoriented other musicians who were simultaneously working out new harmonic approaches. Social forces on a national scale also operated to bring about the new radicalism. The thirties had seen the political awakening of all oppressed and underprivileged people in America. Roosevelt, who stood for "the forgotten man" and who pledged a "New Deal," received a full 75 percent of the Negro vote in 1936. His conscious appeal to the black vote contributed greatly to the new black self-consciousness. Previously, many blacks had argued that they could alter the direction of American policies only through exercising the vote as a group, but the fact remained that previously they had rarely done so. I would suggest, for example, that their ability to act as a group, politically, was to a certain extent predicated on their ability to act as a group *culturally* and that what I have called the *under-*

ground nature of black culture during the thirties was, in fact, the prepolitical organization of black society around cultural specifics. The feeling of strength in numbers, which black society expressed politically in the 1936 election, had been partially generated through black music. Conversely, one can look to the political situation in the latter part of the thirties for clues to the social nature of the radical black music of the forties. The fact remained that Roosevelt's New Deal had failed: the power of government did not change hands in America, nor did the economic structure of the country open significantly to allow the Negro a firmer foothold. Rather, the New Deal served to salvage the pre-Depression economic structure with the large corporations emerging practically unscathed. It was, in fact, the "forgotten man," the average lower-class American, who benefited least, and the Negro who had to bear the added burden of racial discrimination remained fixed to the lowest rung on the socioeconomic ladder.

The sense of strength the black culture had gained during the thirties served only to reinforce its cynicism about American life, and the dubiety of black life in America—with the attraction/repulsion feelings it generated in the average Negro—became more one-sided. The rhythm-and-blues idiom was a sign of overt separation from American society, a return, perhaps, to a kind of pre-urban cultural isolationism brought up-to-date. The jazz idioms, however, particularly the bebop style of playing, expressed a more subtle and more sophisticated approach to the problem. Bop was built on the American tradition that the black man had to prove that he was *better* than the white man on the white man's own terms because only by being better had he been accepted in the past. The black cultural norm was, after all, superior achievement in certain areas of experience. The bop musician began to learn the foundations of Western harmony with a vengeance and to apply them in radically

inventive ways. At the same time, he strove to invent culturally exclusive idioms that were openly hostile to "Uncle
Tomism" and that repelled, by their very nature, both white
musicians and black musicians of middle-class attitude.
Above all else, the bop musician of the forties was against
the status quo: he was for change and against conservatism
in any form. Thus, even as the black musician was struggling to beat the white man at his own game, he was attempting to extend peculiarly black idioms and to clarify cultural distinctions that had been glossed over by traditional
interpretations of the Negro in America. Perhaps the real
significance of this period lay in the black man finally beginning to take the initiative away from the white man, even
in the area of cultural segregation.

The radical black music of the forties was an attempt to
make that separation meaningful. This music was not overtly
racist—that is, there were many white modernists who joined
the musical revolution—but it developed the notion of
"blackness" as a cultural, rather than genetic, condition.
Thus the white musician whose life style, and then whose
music, fitted the revolution was accepted; the black musician
whose life style, and then whose music, was considered
"Uncle Tom" was excluded. Many older Negro players who
could not make the change complained that "These young
guys seem like they want us to die out." The new black musicians were, in fact, "killing their elders," but only in the most
metaphorical sense. They accepted the musical precedents
but not the social orientation of the older Negroes. Stearns
has written that "to allow that the Negro's music should be
granted a role in the world of art leads to disconcerting
questions about who is really cultured in our society."[18]
The bop musicians were, in effect, taking the initiative in
raising that question. In the process, many of the older
Negroes who had accepted Western aesthetic criteria and
social values were sacrificed to the cause.

The black musician, in taking the process of cultural definition into his own hands, infuriated a vast number of whites. Two major trends pointed to the growing hostility of whites toward modern black music. The first was the emergence of the New Orleans "revivalist" movement, which was spearheaded by white "purists" who sought to apply both aesthetic and economic pressure to hold back the growing wave of "modernism." Significantly, the revival of New Orleans type jazz went virtually unnoticed within the urban black community, save for a few oldsters who found themselves back in business after twenty years of retirement. The "revivalist" movement did have its good points—it created a climate for the "mainstream" jazz of the fifties, set European jazz on the path to maturity, and enabled a few really great "primitive" black musicians, like Sidney Bechet, to continue developing. And yet perhaps the most important function of this movement was that it forced the "modernists" to consolidate their position, to shore up their defenses, and to assert themselves more vehemently than before. The second trend was the openly hostile attitude of white music critics, those who did not necessarily support the "revivalist" movement but who were nonetheless violently opposed to bebop. The debate became so fanatic that the influential critic Hugues Panassie went so far as to refer to bop as a "heresy." Panassie's attitude, not uncommon among white critics in the forties, was significant for several reasons. First, it indicated the extent to which some whites had become committed to black music, for to refer to an idiom of black expression as a "heresy" is to imply that alternative idioms of black expression had been accepted as "gospel." Black music had engaged the white listener on an emotional level, and, regardless of the amount of analysis the Western observer applied to jazz, his basic orientation was still emotional. Hence, black music by the forties had become something of a nonideological, secular religion for urban whites as well as blacks. This aspect becomes more crucial as jazz moves into the fifties and sixties. Second, Panassie's attitude was the expression of a basic and profound difficulty that the white man must necessarily bring to black music. Panassie developed his opinions partly around advice given him by older Negro musicians. He was devoutly antiracist and was always falling over backward to assert black "taste" *as he perceived it* with the active support of many of the older black musicians of Harlem. And yet, in the last analysis, it is obvious that he had been misinformed. The point remains that the white intellectual approaching black culture with the best intentions can be, and often is, fooled and that he fools himself further if he thinks he can predict what will and what will not constitute the "taste" or the leadership of black culture. This problem is exaggerated by the Western man's analytic orientation; too often white critics have relied on their intellects rather than on their emotional response to judge black music. Because the oral tradition is not *about* analysis, the Western observer is left open to numerous ploys from opposing factions within black culture. Perhaps Panassie's vehemence was partly a result of some faint awareness that black musicians recognize no formal leadership other than the music itself—the music is the ideology and belongs to the culture as a whole—and that his position was, by definition, highly tenuous to hold and almost impossible to defend.

The hostility facing the bop musicians was also significant in that it brought into the open the hostility between black culture and white value structures that had been dormant for so many years. Again, one can look to misconceptions on the part of white society for clues to the nature of the ensuing hostility. Eric Hobsbaum has suggested that jazz appealed to many middle-class whites particularly because it was a music made by those who, judged "by middle-class ranking," were socially inferior. He continues, "The lady leaves her castle with the raggle-taggle gypsies, not because they play so sweet, but because they are *not* ladies and gentlemen—they are in fact gypsies."[19] Hobsbaum suggests that there is a distinct class system in operation here, but perhaps it would be yet truer to say that it was a matter of cultural orientation rather than actual class distinction. The two concepts are not identical, for although *class* does imply cultural biases through rigid social prestructures, the notion of cultural orientation allows that, while there is considerable fluidity of class in America, there has remained, until very recently, a narrow, white-Anglo-Saxon-Protestant (WASP) ethic, abbreviated here as the Anglo-conformity of American life. But perhaps the conditions of class and culture *are* inseparable: the gypsy music *does* sound sweeter to the emotionally restricted ladies and gentlemen. In either case, it would be fair to say that the young black musicians were, to some extent, reacting to the fact that their music had been accepted by whites partly because they themselves had been relegated to an inferior social position.

This "new" Negro was not just a fabrication of the sentiments of a handful of advanced musicians; in the forties, the social foundations of the bop movement began to be felt everywhere within the black community. The black musician, at the vanguard of that community, was only several years ahead of the times, voicing a sentiment that would grow in time to deafening proportions. World War II had caused even greater upheavals than had the Depression. The issues of racism and democracy, in Harold Isaacs's phrase, "came stamped high and hard on all the circumstances that brought on the power collision of the Second World War." Whereas the Depression did not significantly alter the structure of American society, the Second World War and its aftermath radically altered cultural alliances. "In summoning up the strength to meet the challenge of Hitler and *his* totalitarianism and *his* racism, the Western nations lost their surviving capacity to preserve their own systems of total power in the colonies, their own brands of racism."[20] Several years before American "democracy" had become equated with "anti-Communism," thus allowing old systems of oppression to continue in a new guise, Negroes took the initiative in attempting to realign the old social order.

At home, Negroes were breaking away from traditional interracial alliances. In 1940, for example, 90 percent of the defense contractors hired no Negroes at all. In response, the Negro community, led by A. Philip Randolph, threatened a huge march on Washington. Roosevelt, afraid of the rift this would cause in America, capitulated and signed an executive order banning discrimination in defense work. Ominously, Randolph had said before the capitulation, ". . . we shall not call upon our white friends to march with us. There are some things Negroes must do alone."[21] In the field, Negroes who fought in segregated units until almost the end of the War were clearly "future orientated." A study sponsored by the Army itself indicated that "there was a tendency among Negro soldiers to expect or hope for an increase in rights and privileges, improved treatment, and better economic status after the war."[22] A main motivation behind the Negro's enthusiasm to "prove himself as American as the next guy" had been the conscious belief that America would warm to his domestic cause after the War. When he returned home to find the usual lack of work, and discrimination returned both to the military forces and to the defense industries, the lower-class black became even more reluctant to allow the white establishment to define his goals or program his actions. The great Detroit race riot of 1943 in which twenty-five blacks and nine whites died and $2 million in damage was caused, spoke vividly of a hostility toward American social structure that was no longer dormant. This riot thoroughly shocked American society which had been unaware of the depth and breadth of black disaffection from

the American status quo. The riot was a spontaneous eruption of black aggression, coordinated and regulated by the
"collective unconscious" of the lower-class black community,
without formal leadership from either middle-class spokes-
men such as Randolph or lower-class messiahs such as
Garvey.

The innovations of bop musicians were rhythmic as well as
harmonic and thus had a direct effect on the quality of social
action within the black culture, as rhythmic advances have
been seen to be both a cause and a function of social freedom.
Charles "Bird" Parker was a genius of rhythmic invention.
Like Armstrong and Young before him, he invented techniques to solve problems not uniquely his own. Parker, more
than Armstrong perhaps, proved that it was expedient to
solve problems posed by Western form—i.e., the harmonic
structure of Western music—through the application of oral
techniques. In the process, he raised blues playing to a true
art, using "internal hearing" and musical intuition to arrive
at chord manipulations that startled even the most "educated" Western musicians. Many black musicians had become serious students of Western harmonic form by the
early forties, and several, like trumpet player Dizzy Gillespie
and drummer Kenny Clarke, had become fairly accomplished
piano players as well. Yet Parker's advances were qualitatively unlike Gillespie's, although the two influenced each
other greatly. Gillespie himself acknowledges a basic difference. Parker had more of the anguish and lyricism of the
blues in his tone which was always one of the most powerful
elements of his playing, whereas Gillespie appeared to regard
tone as secondary to harmonic invention. Parker proved
that the two could be functions of each other and cultivated
the "cry" in his sound. Born and raised in Kansas City, he
had played with Jay McShann's blues-oriented band for
several years before coming to New York; it was therefore
no surprise that he often sounded very close to the melisma

of the rougher blues singers. His runs on the horn would go by so fast they were like a vocal smear, a moan or a cry. The startling fact is that when one slows down his 33 rpm records to 16 rpm, it is evident that those smears are actually complex and perfectly articulated structures of advanced Western harmony, with an added element of "the accidental" that is closer to magic than to mastery of technique.

Parker's incredible technical facility on the instrument —the speed with which he could execute runs and the breakneck tempos at which he was able to sustain creativity—was only half of his advantage, for the source of his melodic "magic" was his ability to "hear internally" a new harmonic conception before anybody had written it out as a formal theory. He describes the very moment of breakthrough: "I'd been getting bored with the stereotyped changes that were being used at the time, and I kept thinking there's bound to be something else. *I could hear it sometimes but I couldn't play it* [my emphasis]. Well, that night, I was working over 'Cherokee,' and, as I did, I found that by using the higher intervals of a chord as a melody line and backing them with appropriately related changes, *I could play the thing I'd been hearing* [my emphasis again]."[23] Parker's lyricism, then, came directly out of his conception of melody, relegating harmonic construction to a "backing" role, and his arrival at this conception through "internal hearing" and, not incidentally, blues playing. Gillespie's harmonies, just as advanced as Parker's, had been "worked out" at a piano keyboard and this made them qualitatively different. This distinction, verbalized, seems very tenuous but because the piano keyboard allows one to visualize Western harmony— to translate abstract intervals, with all their potential for vocalization, into rigid, physical intervals—it remains subtle in terms of musical conception. Parker's advances were reputed to be so strongly rooted in the common language of his culture that "he'd play a phrase, and people might never have heard it before, but he'd start it, and the people would finish it with him, humming. It would be so lyrical and simple that it just seemed the most natural thing to play."[24] Although Parker had his clichés, he was not a repetitious player, and the ability of the crowd to "finish phrases" with him can be explained only in terms of a common *cultural conception* of melody and lyricism. By the sixties, black musicians were eschewing all formal (i.e., keyboard, technique in an attempt at tapping this cultural source, which is the spontaneous, nonanalytic nature of the oral tradition.

Parker's records became classics overnight. His version of "Parker's Mood" remains the quintessence of bop style blues playing, and his ballad playing, or his "love" music as he called it, built searing structures on the most mundane popular material. By using standard chord changes, such as the banal "I Got Rhythm" sequence, Parker elevated the popular culture of the day to the point where it was often considered art. His playing also caused a revolution in the rhythmic approach of other musicians. Drummer Max Roach has said, "Even the way I play drums, you can say Bird was really responsible. Not just because his style called for a particular kind of drumming, but because he set tempos so fast, it was impossible to play straight."[25] To free the time feeling and allow Parker room for his solos, piano players also had to change their way of playing—they developed a style of "feeding" the saxophonist chord changes and played brief, percussive accents. The rhythmic feel was augmented through the application of this "space" concept by drummers. With Kenny Clarke at the lead, bop drummers played the "time"—the steady $\frac{4}{4}$ feeling—on the ride cymbal, creating a steady "sizzle," or high-frequency drone effect, using the rest of their drum kit to add rhythmic accents or propulsions. Clarke's style of drumming was called "tipping" because when he and a bass player worked together, "it sounded like they were rushing," but in reality the time was steady: the "part of the beat" they played—like that employed by the Kansas City musicians who moved away from "on the beat" playing—gave the emotional feeling of acceleration. Yet this feeling was much more free than the "ride" or "push" of the thirties' rhythm sections. Parker's technical facility changed jazz from a music built on quarter and eighth notes to one built on sixteenth and thirty-second notes and pushed jazz improvisation beyond the limits of bar line restrictions or those of chord cycles to a new plateau of rhythmic freedom. Gradually, the time feel came to be implied rather than stated, absorbed into the group feel and removed from the heavy bar line accents of "swing" drummers. Parker developed devices to pull off this effect and to help educate other musicians to the possibilities it opened up. For example, he would "start on the 11th bar, and as the rhythm section stayed where they were and [he] played where he was, it sounded as if the rhythm section was on one and three instead of two and four." Miles Davis refers to this as "turning the rhythm section around."[26]

Russell has said of bop rhythm that it "differs from swing rhythm, because it is more complex and places greater emphasis upon polyrhythms. It differs emotionally from swing rhythm, creating greater tension, thereby reflecting more accurately the spirit and temper of contemporary emotions."[27] Russell's recognition of the association of the rhythmic feel of black music and the social climate is apt, particularly in light of the fact that the connection between rhythmic advances and social change is always very tight in the oral culture. Indeed, there were several signs that black musicians were beginning to cultivate oral techniques consciously, for their own sake. This was evident in the rhythm-and-blues music, as well as in the increasingly fashionable place occupied by Afro-Cuban music within black communities. Some say that the interest in Afro-Cuban music was a response to an increased international consciousness of the American Negro, associated with the emergence of black African nations and the formation of the United Nations. Jones has suggested that the most important aspect of the music of the forties was "its reassertion of many 'non-Western' concepts of music. Certainly the reestablishment of the hegemony of polyrhythms are much closer to a purely African way of making music, than they are to any Western concepts."[28] But it should be suggested that the reassertion of techniques peculiar to an oral, black American culture does not necessarily indicate a conscious reexamination of African orality. The external causes for the shake-up in lower-class black culture that have been suggested were more probably the source for the rhythmic advances than were overt "Africanisms." A few black musicians made the trip to Africa to find "the source," but even *their* music remained thoroughly American.

By 1945, Parker and Gillespie's small 52nd Street group challenged the supremacy of the big band sound. They played extended improvisation in difficult keys to separate the serious musicians from the "no talent guys." This extended improvisation was no longer casual, as it had been during the thirties; small groups were fighting for economic survival in New York, and the musicians there were in deadly earnest about their music. Because of the climate that had surrounded swing music, these musicians first sought to isolate themselves from the "non-serious" listener. Many bop musicians were quoted at various times as saying, "I don't care if you listen to my music or not," a far cry from the entertainers' posture developed by Armstrong and his contemporaries during the twenties. As Stearns indicated, the Negro was refusing to play the stereotyped role of *entertainer,* which he associated with "Uncle Tomism." "He then proceeded to play the most revolutionary jazz with an appearance of utter boredom, rejecting his audience entirely."[29]

He may have done so out of a desire to be judged on the merits of his music alone—the new seriousness tended to disregard the virtues of jazz as a quasi-folk art—and in the process actually enchanted his audience. For, in truth, the part of the audience not alienated by indifferent stage mannerisms became more committed to the music the less the musician paid attention to them. The extreme scene tended to glorify the music. The audience was reacting to the musician's *stance,* just as that stance had become a large part of the bop musician's music. The radical young black players lifted jazz out of the life of the middle-class American, whether white or black. They had discovered the strength of confrontation tactics: in times of social flux, the boldest, most aggressive social posture is more beneficial to the "cause," and hence to the individual, than is compromise, if only because implacability can never be construed as weakness.

The psychological conflicts within the black musician were just as important as any social movements. Unlike the rhythm-and-blues player who had reacted to the demand for cultural consolidation by aiming his music *away* from white society, the black jazz musician tried to project his music *over the head* of the average white listener. As the swing music of the thirties became accepted by the white middle-class (that class which had never had any overt interest in jazz), black jazz players strove even harder to separate themselves and their music from mainstream America. A new "serious" attitude, often taking comic turns as in Gillespie's high camp imitations of Western intellectuals, surrounded the bop musicians. And yet, the only precedent for a "serious" music, or musician's attitude, available to them was that of the classical Western music tradition built on an entirely different performer/audience relationship than jazz. This left the bop musicians free to invent new modes of "serious" conduct and "serious" music, yet never quite able to break free of conventional notions of classical Western intellectualism.

Although Parker's was a "musician's music," that is, although it was addressed to peer group musicians first and to an audience of laymen and critics second, he was sensitive to the reactions of the music establishment. In his search for "respectability" within the serious world of Western music, he had gone to visit composer Edgard Varèse just before his death and begged, "Take me as you would a baby and teach me music. I only write in one voice. I want to write orchestral scores."[30] Parker and his associates had been listening to classical music and greatly admired the harmonic structure of Western modernists. This music was the only "serious" tradition they knew of, and they wanted to enter it. They had turned their back on critical acceptance, but they were unable to sever completely the ties with Western criteria of legitimacy. They were psychologically unable to declare, as black musicians would during the sixties, that because Western tradition *denied* certain aspects of black tradition, it was perhaps necessary verbally to deny Western tradition. Cecil Taylor, for example, when asked about his "classical training" said, "I am like hell classically trained." He continued to explain that his biggest problem as a pianist was learning how to forget what he had been "taught." Although it was primarily a musical consideration, Parker's desire to write orchestral scores was not an uncommon social theme during the forties. Bud Powell, too, had made plans with members of the faculty of the Juilliard School of Music to compose orchestral versions of his music. The drive to be recognized as an artist—to be taken seriously—by the Western establishment hints at the basic insecurity of the urban Negro's life. The music of both Parker and Powell was, in fact, highly structured but intuitively rather than formally. Their desire to "compose" was one with their desire to have the merits of their intuition corroborated and legitimized by the music establishment or at least to have this establishment cease ignoring their musical contributions. One reason this corroboration was not forthcoming was that the music establishment, as a body, could not come to grips with the social implications of recognizing black music as "art." Although individual modern composers often recognized that bebop was the first instance of popular Western music transcending the restrictions of the diatonic scale, still bebop remained a musical idiom built on Tin Pan Alley song forms, i.e., the 12-, 16-, and 32-bar constructions. That is, bebop remained *popular* music. To allow this radical new popular music into the realm of "art" not only called into question just who was really cultured in American society, but also the *place* of music, and "art" in general, in social organization. Although the music itself spoke of serious investigations, the demeanor of the musicians and the audience who produced the music simply did not fit into the traditional Western mold of *serious behavior*. Because their social conduct was inextricably tied to the social nature of peculiarly black music, the bebop musicians became hypersensitive to racial issues in general. I suggest, then, that the drive for white respectability ultimately became, in part, one with the need to confront the white man over the issue of racism.

The original mode of black protest in America—it was adopted by the earliest slaves and became part of the Negro's self-image—was one of disengagement from mainstream American life. During slavery, apathy was one of the few socially acceptable weapons of defense and even after Emancipation remained the most important mode of resistance. Whereas mainstream America had told the emancipated Negro, "It is important *how* you play the game," the Negro, particularly after the failure of Reconstruction, had begun to speculate that it was perhaps more important whether or not one chose to play the game at all: "It doesn't matter if you win or lose but *if* you play the game." The basic posture of black protest in America, then, resembles apathy but is actually more like self-conscious isolationism. It was not articulated as such by the Negro, however, until the "underground" movement that grew out of the thirties and into the forties. Parker's generation, having intuitively recognized that the ground rules were stacked against them, was the first to declare the "game" not worth playing and so became the first to articulate isolationism in a socially aggressive manner. The shock troops that paved the road for the mass movements during the fifties and sixties appear, in retrospect, to have been overly self-conscious in their social posturing. Yet Parker and his group of musicians did develop a conscious social style based on isolationism from the ground rules of the Western "game."

Robert Reisner has said of Parker that "Bird was the supreme hipster. He made his own laws. His arrogance was enormous, his humility profound."[31] The "hip" ethic, which grew out of an articulation of the social style of the bop musicians, maintained the principle of cultural isolation but also tried to turn the denial of mainstream culture into a positive posture. Kerouac's treatment of this life style (in *On the Road* particularly) and the work of the existentialists (Sartre and Camus especially) are white parallels: attempts at verbalizing similar kinds of social posture. At the root of the hip ethic is an almost arrogant assertion of individuality, a fight for personal integrity in the face of growing urban depersonalization and the rejection of the stifling inhibitions of Western society. The hipster sought to escape from the guilt and anxiety that perpetuates the "work ethic" of Anglo-conformity, and the techniques he adopted were all geared toward this end. He rarely tried to articulate his position to the "square"; in fact, he seemed not to want to discuss the question of what the hip ethic was all about. This ethic had become axiomatic to its followers and was certainly not in need of justification. "Hipness is not a state of mind," one black musician has said, "it is a fact of life." There was no racial inference in the hip ethic, only cultural inferences, the assertion of a particular style of individualized expression, originating within the black culture, over and against mass conformity. Of course, this kind of nonconformity became in time a kind of conformity in itself, especially when it was adopted by many whites who had little cultural precedent for the kind of social improvisation practiced within the oral tradition. Black musicians were using the term *hippie* twenty-five years ago as a term of derision for the false, or pseudo, hipster. The hip ethic spread throughout black and white America as an almost subconscious message of the new music. Those whites seeking a vehicle of nonconformity within mainstream America naturally gravitated toward the hip subculture. By the end of the forties, the black "underground" was becoming increasingly multiracial in membership if not in character.

The hipster used a complex vocabulary, taken from the language of music. This convention is still current to some extent. Morris has suggested that any set of jargon serves to isolate those who use it. He has written that "it is easy to see how the anti-communication function of language has been almost as important as its communication function. More than any social custom, it has set up enormous intergroup barriers. More than anything else, it has identified an individual . . . and put obstacles in the way of his defecting to another group."[32] In the case of hip jargon, language was used to minimize the importance of previously established social barriers. But, behind the recognition of cultural barriers, there was always the shadow of the racial barrier. Hip whites could never fully identify with black culture, although many tried.[33] Whites brought a different set of experiences and perceptual orientations to the language. Moreover, when a facet or phrase of black, or hip, jargon gained too much currency within the white world, it was summarily dropped by blacks. This suggests that a "secret" language functions differently within the black community than it does without, or, at least, that hip jargon is part of the Negro's drive for an "ethnically singular" voice. At its most elementary, in-group language is simply a means of easy communication to integrate shared experience into its semantics and thereby exclude those who do not share a background. In the black community, as in the vernacular of other oppressed groups, it also serves as an emotional release, a means of softening the impact of oppression or of obscuring overt resistance to oppression. It served a double function: it rendered white America incommunicado in the context of the ghettos at the same time that it rendered the black man harmless—or seemingly so—in the context of white society.

Grier and Cobbs have suggested that "starting with slavery, black people, and more particularly black men, have had to devise ways of expressing themselves uniquely and individually and in a manner that was not threatening to the white man . . . an important aspect of his containment is the fear that his aggression will be directed against the white world and will bring swift punishment."[34] Thus, the "cool" musical style the bebop musicians were said, and indeed sometimes claimed, to have developed was, in fact, not passive at all. Audiences, critics, and even musicians outside the movement assumed that because the black musician turned his back on an audience or because he wore a look of boredom, he actually felt detached. The style of the bop musicians, however, grew out of great inner turmoil. The "cool" posture was not a reflection of passivity but, rather, of actionality turned inward: the active repression of very basic emotional turbulence for fear it would turn outward to mainstream America and invite retribution. "Playing it cool" becomes significant as it becomes apparent that it is effected at substantial cost and suffering. The hipster raised to a "high art" a life style that was peculiarly a product of black American tradition. This accounts for the obvious anguish in Parker's playing as he consciously "turned his back" on those who paid to hear him play. The repression of deeply felt emotion becomes, itself, a deeply felt emotion. As black culture went consciously underground in America, as it struck the pose of overt rejection of American norms, its appeal to the white community changed. Previously, black culture had been thought of as a "harmless" kind of popular culture. The rhythm-and-blues idioms did little, at first, to alter this view. But the bop idiom and the hip ethic were clearly posed alternatives to the American way of life and to Western value structures. Thus, they became all the more attractive to those whites who were gradually becoming disenchanted with Western value structures and all the more a threat to the American establishment. The popularity of black music among young whites—whether it was the bop of the forties or the rhythm-and-blues of the fifties—was an indication of the disaffection that lay behind the political activism of the sixties. Mailer's term *the white Negro* is accurate, as is his conception of a value transfer from black culture to whites through idioms such as black music and speech patterns.

Critical to the process of cultural isolation during the forties was the increasingly widespread use of heroin among black musicians. Parker had been using heroin since the age of twelve, and his influence as a musician spread throughout the lower-class Negro culture in proportion, it seemed, to the use of this drug.[35] All illegal drugs, irrespective of their physiological effects, tend to isolate the user from mainstream society in that they make him an outlaw. Heroin, however, was particularly suited to the passive front of the black musician because it chemically suppressed aggressive feelings and allayed anxieties. It was also suited to the displacement of social involvement because it involved the user in a perpetual social cycle of either searching for the drug or being "laid out" behind its effects. Heroin spoke kindly to the "cool" style of the hipster for three reasons: it suppresses emotional excess; it establishes an in-group of users and dealers; and it eases anxieties not directly concerned with procuring it. Drugs have always been part of the music scene in black America, but one must distinguish between the use of marijuana, and even the extreme abuse of alcohol, and heroin addiction. The latter, unlike marijuana, creates physical dependence and unlike alcohol is socially unacceptable. Its very destructiveness, however, caters to the assertion of the individual's will in a most peculiar way: every heroin user knows that the odds are against him—that he will become addicted in time—and yet he tends to maintain the unreasonable belief that he alone is strong enough to beat these odds. Heroin also alters aural perception in the user. Although Parker himself said that anybody who claimed to play better under the influence of any drug was "a plain straight liar," the empirical evidence, as Art Blakey has said, is that "although you do not play better with heroin, you do hear better."[36] Heroin is therefore ironically suited to involvement with aural/oral culture.

Blakey has said that Parker "wanted to kick the habit so that he could tell people what he heard. It was something like a neurotic. While he is suffering, he cannot produce; but reflecting about his pain, he can create. Musicians who have been junkies and then rid themselves of the habit have sometimes really then come into their own musically."[37] There is some truth to Blakey's assessment. Particularly during the late fifties, several black musicians did kick the habit permanently and then fulfilled their potential. More common, however, was the junkie who is constantly kicking, who gets "clean" only to become a heavy user again. Perhaps Blakey's insight is sound: perhaps heroin is part of the creative process in general. But one must be skeptical, for there is clearly a surfeit of sources for creative stimulus within the black culture without resorting to the narcissism of heroin addiction. Archie Shepp's summation is to the point: "Scag (heroin) ain't dope, it's death!" If heroin has any advantage for the black musician it is in the perceptual sphere, to the extent that it allows one to "hear better" and in the social sphere, to the extent that it consolidates black culture against white norms and makes of the user an overt, rather than a covert, outlaw.

By the end of the forties, the hip ethic had become a kind of recondite social philosophy of some magnitude which held as its basic tenet that "squares" were the true "outsiders" and that hipsters alone knew "where it was at." This was a long-standing "inside" feeling among jazz musicians, and it is only the fact that it took hold within both the black and white communities—outside the realm of music—that makes it a significant social phenomenon.[38] This reversal of norms wherein the social deviant sees the greater public as not only uninformed but potentially dangerous was an advance over the acceptance of second-class citizenship, particularly for Negroes. The fifties and sixties saw the evolution of the hip ethic from social curiosity to substantial social influence. The hipster's roots in the black "underground" assured the black culture a vanguard role in the American social revolution, and his association with black music, never a casual one, remained central to the development of that revolution.

The year 1947 seems an appropriate point at which to end the discussion of the formative stages of contemporary black underground culture. That year, the famed 52nd Street, where most of the new jazz was being played, closed down for all practical purposes, presumably because of high-pressure techniques by the management—high cover charges and small tables—and the corruption of the white middle-class youths by prostitutes and drug users. (The clubs were replaced by burlesque houses.) The management also claimed that the musicans' agents had priced the jazzmen out of work. Ironically, it was during this year that Parker was playing at one of his creative peaks, using a group that included Max Roach and, occasionally, Bud Powell. His Dial recordings of this period, featuring Miles Davis, Duke Jordan, Tommy Potter, and Roach, were as influential as Armstrong's Hot Five recordings had been. In 1947, too, the NAACP presented the United Nations Office of Social Affairs with a 155-page document with the lengthy title *A Statement on the Denial of Human Rights to Minorities in the Case of Citizens of Negro Descent in the United States of America and an Appeal to the United Nations for Redress*. Clearly, even the black middle-class, represented by the NAACP, was searching for ways to confront America's racial, and thus cultural, establishment. The importance of the bop musician was that he had achieved this confrontation—in terms of aesthetics and value structures as well as social action—well before organized legal or political action. Further, unlike the arguments of the NAACP, his music and his hip ethic were not subject to the kind of rationalization and verbal qualification that had all too often compromised out of existence all middle-class Negro gains.

5

Black Visibility:
1949–1969

The National Advisory Commission on Civil Disorders, or the "riot commission" as it was called, was established by President Johnson after the long hot summer of 1967 to look into the causes of the racial disturbances. The commission's report published in 1968 was summarily ignored by President Johnson who along with millions of other Americans bridled at the findings: "Our nation is moving toward two societies, one white, one black—separate and unequal. . . . The most fundamental [cause of the riots] is the racial attitude and behavior of white Americans toward black Americans. . . . White racism is essentially responsible for the explosive mixture which has been accumulating in our cities since the end of World War Two."[1] The gathering explosive mixture, moreover, was a function of black migration as well: between 1950 and 1965, 5.5 million Negroes migrated from the South to the urban areas of the North and West. The increased migration did not create a better atmosphere for integration but actually furthered the separation of the two cultures. This fact was coldly substantiated by one demographic survey, conducted by a major news magazine, which concluded that the "white Middle American, out of perversity or ignorance, is convinced that Negroes actually have a better chance to get ahead in America than he does and that any troubles blacks suffer are probably their own fault."[2] Likewise, the "riot commission" report, although it suggested that white America was perfectly capable of reading history, remained blind to the primary cultural causes of the separation, and this blindness was amplified throughout the white community.

Since, as I have suggested, America had been moving toward "two societies" for decades, the importance of the "riot commission" report was not so much in its specific findings as in its recognition of an alteration in the *articulated* relationship between black and white Americans. White society had always *attributed* such and such a character to black culture in America. During slavery, the Negro had been considered "harmless," "childlike," and somehow "carefree," and this image survived well into the twentieth century, modified occasionally as during the twenties when it was enlarged to include the qualities of "hedonism" and "innocence" in the face of urban, industrial life. The black man had remained invisible to the extent that he did not agree with this attributed image and yet remained silent. Beginning in the fifties, however, American Negroes began to *project* an image they deemed favorable, and by the sixties, this self-defined image was running quite contrary to previously accepted images. This was basically an urban phenomenon where blacks were feeling strength in numbers and were gaining psychological freedom from Southern stereotypes. I have suggested that this was, in fact, a central theme among black musicians during the forties; I further suggest that because the black musician is in the cultural vanguard of the black community, the new visibility of the fifties and sixties was both a result of his earlier activities and a reaffirmation of his leadership status.

Yet the major trend in modern black music, that of the postwar era, has been its acceptance by major segments of white America—an acceptance on several levels of experience and in as many ways as there were individuals involved.

Black music, in short, became part of the experience—and the vocabulary—of mainstream America during the last quarter-century. The effects of the oral psychology were often rejected outright—as we have seen in the case of the "middle American"—and, perhaps less often but equally as significant, were also accepted outright and with passion by the white radicals. At no time, however, certainly not after the explosive sixties, could white America avoid confronting the issue.

During the sixties, a pamphlet entitled *The Student as Nigger* circulated on major college campuses in the United States. A few years before, black militants had exhorted the young white radicals to join in calling middle-class whites "honkies," on the basis that whiteness was a state of mind not a fact of birth; now this pamphlet urged that blackness was a fact of culture and that young whites had gained a certain fluency from it. Hence, the white population has become polarized during the past two decades partly over the issue of cultural orientation. In a sense, the issue of "civil rights" was a smoke screen that obscured this fact, and the move within the black community away from it and toward "human rights," and the growing sentiment within that community that integration was perhaps more racist than segregation all pointed to the true *cultural* basis of the issues. What was at stake was not the black man's individual rights; it was, rather, the more general limitation through cultural suppression of an individual's freedom. Freedom, in this sense, is not something which can be granted; it can only be denied. It is usually denied under the camouflage of vast cultural prejudices or national priorities. A statement issued by the National Council of Churches seemed to recognize this: "We are faced with a situation where powerless conscience meets conscienceless power, threatening the very foundation of our Nation. . . . America has asked its Negro citizens to fight for opportunity as *individuals,* whereas at certain points in our history what we have needed most has been opportunity for the *whole group,* not just for selected and approved Negroes."[3] This statement further recognized that black culture can and does act as a kind of "cultural conscience" for all Americans. Inasmuch as black music itself provides a secular but nonetheless spiritual foundation through basic oral orientation, this "cultural conscience" is perhaps closely related to the "collective unconscious" generated through black musical idioms. Young whites had heard black music several years before the "civil rights" movement captured the imaginations of liberal Americans. Black music, then, was at least part of the basic "cause" that changed the young American "rebel without a cause" into a political activist.

The urbanization of the past two decades in America has seen the final stages in the secularization of black culture. One black musician summarized the feelings of many: "I stopped going to church. It was too much to take, man. . . . What you wanna do, go to church and cry each Sunday? See, you feel *too* much. When people feel a lot, man, that's like Trane [John Coltrane] or any black artist, that's how they project their music." We were listening to a gospel record at the time, and he continued about the singer: "You know, she's talking about 'when I get to heaven.' Now where is heaven at, man? You know? Maybe she believed in that shit but she get out on that road and find out something else. And she'll turn it into a blues thing. None of that shit don't matter. You can cry in church all day long, go home and tell the rent man you ain't got any money."

The financial difficulties of urban life began to force the Negro to confront the cultural biases of America's economic institutions. One musician, who years before had told me he was going to continue to play professionally and had then gone on to work with the biggest "names" in jazz, had quit the profession altogether. "No, I wasn't talking money *then,*" he said, "but I'm in New York City now and I done found out how much money it takes to live. I can't make any money at this point playing creative music, music of *today,* so I'm gonna stop wasting my time, cause I figure don't many of us have that much of it left." This feeling that the cultural war had finally come, or was swiftly coming, to a head, corresponded to the feelings of white radicals.

Unlike the upsurge of hedonism that followed World War I, the social climate of America following World War II was deceptively passive. Even the black culture which had consolidated during the forties maintained a "wait-and-see" attitude toward the American experience. This attitude was reflected in all the black music up until the middle fifties. Inasmuch as very little in the way of social or material gains was immediately forthcoming, the passivity quickly took on a more deviant characteristic. Heroin use, because it complemented this "wait-and-see" attitude, increased geometrically in the years following the war—and with this increase, the cool ethic became formalized, stylized, and synthesized. The gang fighting that had been the major status activity among black youth during the forties gave way to heroin use as the ultimate status activity. As Claude Brown reports, "It was time to stop smoking reefers and stop drinking wine; it was time to start really getting high."[4] Widespread heroin use, moreover, had political implications. White authorities turned their backs on the problem as long as it remained confined to the black ghettos, most probably because heroin users are ostensibly passive and the social damage they do do, i.e., thefts and burglaries, is usually within the ghetto itself. The lack of white concern during the fifties was itself a kind of negative political statement, telling the Negroes to take care of their own. On the other hand, as Howard Brotz has indicated, ". . . alienation from the established conventions and opinions of society—no matter how indifferent these established opinions may seem from an impartial standpoint—can never be wholly politically neutral."[5] The use of heroin inasmuch as it was overtly deviant in terms of established conventions carried with it political overtones, albeit on a broad, cultural wavelength.

Moreover, heroin use was gradually becoming associated with a new style of black masculinity created, essentially, by the black musician. The junkie was first of all participating in the latest "hip" fashion, introduced by the musician archetype during the forties. He was also seeking a shortcut to the presentation of a masculine "front": the drug caused a "drag" in the user's voice. "It made you sound like a real gangster or like a real old cat. And everybody wanted to sound old."[6] This drive for a masculine front was part of a new sense of community within the black ghettos, based on the notion of ultramasculinity. One indication as to the nature of this community spirit was the use of the hip nominative "baby," introduced by black musicians. Calling a friend "baby" implied, "Man, look at me. I've got masculinity to spare. . . . I can say 'baby' to another cat and he can say 'baby' to me, and we can say it with strength in our voices. If you could say it, this meant that you were really sure of your masculinity."[7] Only blacks could use the term effectively, could "give it the meaning that we all knew it had without ever mentioning it—the meaning of black masculinity."

The stasis and apparent ennui of the early fifties, then, took place against this backdrop of deceptive passivity, the growing sense of community within the black culture around the notion of masculine assertion. The mood of the period was partly captured in the Miles Davis/Gil Evans recording, later issued as an LP caled *Birth of the Cool*. In terms of Davis's total output to date, this record represents only one small facet of his playing, one brief stage in the evolution of black consciousness. The "cool," or mood of stasis, of this record was achieved through the use of a nine-piece band, as opposed to the generally accepted bop quintet, made up of wind instruments and brass plus a rhythm section that remained very much in the background. A tuba replaced the more volatile string bass and achieved a fluid rhythmic motion; significantly, the drums, too, played a minor supporting role. In fact, it is possible to listen to this record and imagine that the total effect would be the same if there were no drums used at all. The lack of rhythmic propulsion indicated the guarded nature of the black community, inasmuch as rhythmic assertion had always characterized black cultural assertion. Gil Evans had been working along with Gerry Mulligan on arrangements for the white Claude Thornhill, leader of a harmonically advanced but rhythmically reticent big band. Davis, who is basically a romantic player, found in Evans's work a vehicle for the expression of his romanticism and for post-Parker harmonic innovation without having to state the rhythmic priorities that later became central to his music. The feeling of this record is markedly different from the free-fall feeling of the bop quintets. The music seems to float, an effect achieved through the harmonic textures. The result, Evans was to say later, "had a hypnotic effect." In its purest form, that of the Thornhill band, this approach "could put you to sleep . . . [Thornhill] liked the stationary effect so much, in fact, that if he could have had his way, I think he would have had the band hold one chord for one hundred bars. . . ."[8] The effect was not unlike a drone, wherein all chords become relative to a dominant tonal center, and the only movement is that of the soloist, an area that both Davis and John Coltrane explored years later.

The *Birth of the Cool* record was taken up by many white musicians as a standard perhaps because it relied on harmonic invention (the Western element) rather than rhythmic strength. These players, led by Mulligan, went on to pioneer a jazz idiom alternatively called "West Coast," or "Cool," jazz. Played primarily by white Californians—the location may be significant because California is geographically as far away from Harlem as one can get within the continental United States—this idiom was a rapprochement with Western music. It was also, to some extent, a return to the counterpoint of "Dixieland" music. John Graas has suggested that Mulligan's main contribution to the idiom was "to bring jazz dynamics down to the dynamic range of a string bass—and then to use counterpoint in a natural, unschooled way."[9] Mulligan's reintroduction of the pianoless group was just as important in the hands of Ornette Coleman and Sonny Rollins several years later; it freed the soloist from rhythmic and harmonic restrictions and made possible a style of black music which was the very antithesis of "West Coast" jazz. Mulligan's "modernism," like that of the Davis/Evans collaboration, was an extension of Parker's exploration of the harmonic aspects of jazz, the most Western facet of a hybrid idiom. Mulligan's Western orientation was basic to his music; whereas original New Orleans counterpoint had been "loud" and "rough"—the elements that related it to the blues tradition—Mulligan's style was soft and precise.

The extraordinary success of "West Coast" jazz, along with that of Dave Brubeck's "modern" quartet and Stan Kenton's "progressive" big band (all primarily white organizations), ultimately did affect black musicians although their initial reaction was indifference. One of the few successful black "modern" groups, the Modern Jazz Quartet, made surprisingly little impression on the community of black musicians. In fact, many black players began lamenting that John Lewis, the group's musical director, used to swing but he "don't any more." Ultimately, the MJQ was convinced by Gunther Schuller to join a string section and to play a musical contrivance called "Third Stream" jazz. The "first stream," or Western classical tradition, was to be synthesized with the "second stream," or jazz tradition, to create a new

"Third Stream." Although their reliance on Western music did not approach the rather sinister denigration of black music found in such syntheses as Paul Whiteman's "melodious advances," the "Third Stream" formula did carry with it the notion that black music somehow *improved* as it responded to Western techniques. Indeed, Western music was considered the *first* stream, i.e., the primary one. John Lewis, when I interviewed him in 1963, was enthusiastic about this approach, but Milt Jackson, the member of the quartet most firmly committed to the blues idiom, was openly hostile to what the group was doing. He became somewhat notorious several years later when the press discovered that he had recorded *The Ballad Artistry of Milt Jackson,* a lush, highly romantic album with strings, while watching a baseball game on a portable television he had brought into the studio with him! Clearly there was a disparity between what his audience demanded and what he preferred to play.

The success of these "modern" groups had a broader, more indirect effect on black musicians than the immediate reaction of distaste. As Nathan Hare has noted, ". . . the public definition of a social movement may affect it in unanticipated ways."[10] As the role of jazz musician became more acceptable to the white middle class, it began to lose some of its luster within the black lower class; this foreshadowed the increasing importance of the black rhythm-and-blues musician, who remained anathema to the white middle class well into the sixties. Black jazz musicians continued to produce "art for people's sake" rather than "art for art's sake," and the white middle class was becoming more willing to consider itself part of "the people."

That critical acceptance of jazz during the fifties had taken some of the sting out of the black jazzman's challenge to white values was substantiated in a study by Princeton sociologist Edward Harvey. He found "an increased positive valuation of jazz music by the general public" had caused the "deviant ideology and practices which have previously been reported as characterizing the group [jazz musicians]" to diminish.[11] Yet Harvey's study also shows that jazz musicians under the age of thirty-five were twice as conscious of racial prejudice in the profession than were those over the age of thirty-five. Harvey does not indicate the racial mix of his subject group, but the increased racial consciousness of the younger musicians parallels what had become a significant trend as early as the mid-fifties. Because the public had become more amenable to jazz idioms that were specifically Westernized, black musicians initiated a resurgence of the least-Westernized aspects of the idiom. The fact that the deviant ideology of jazz musicians *as a whole* was on the wane indicated a growing influx of white middle-class musicians into the jazz profession. The younger black musicians who made up an ever smaller proportion of those who could be considered "jazz" musicians were becoming increasingly militant about their blackness. Indeed, the stress of oral orientation within the dominant literate culture is often, itself, enough to satisfy the criteria of deviance within American society. Thus, in terms of the younger black musicians, Harvey's conclusions about diminishing deviance among jazz musicians are misleading. For example, one effect of white acceptance of black idioms was the creation of new forms of "aesthetic deviance" and new criteria for "serious" music. Thus, the "positive valuation" of jazz in the early fifties by whites actually lent authority to future, peculiarly black forms of "deviant" expression.

The new black assertiveness emerged about 1955 with the rise of the "soul" mystique. Just as unfavorable critical reaction to black music during the forties had been used to the advantage of bop musicians, so too the favorable critical reaction to predominantly white idioms of jazz spawned new black idioms. The "soul" phenomenon must be approached from several angles. There was a strong sociological foundation for this movement. On May 17, 1954, the Supreme Court in the *Brown v. Board of Education* decision, reading the final requiem for the style of social segregation that had grown out of the *Plessy v. Ferguson* decision, ruled that "separate educational facilities are *inherently* unequal." The new ruling recognized that any distinctly two-culture society in America maintained an *inherent* subjugation of one culture to the other, a theme that would be picked up later in the "riot commission" report. The boost this decision brought to black confidence is inestimable. It brought on what Isaacs has called "a loss of fear." One Negro leader he interviewed reported: "How this came about I don't know but there is no question about it. The fear posture of the Negro has changed very markedly. . . . Indians say this is what Gandhi did for them, to make them lose their fear, to stop cringing."[12] The roots of this loss of fear go well beyond the growing sense of a "masculine" community that appeared within black ghettos as early as 1950. The American Negro after 1954, however, began to draw strength from the fact that his country's legal structure had, for the first time, publicly admitted the validity of the black man's cause and was prepared to make accommodations. For the first time in black American history, it seemed *possible* that history had turned in favor of even the poorest black and that he could *do* something to advance himself.

"Soul" music, then, was one origin of a cultural self-improvement program and, in insisting the Negro had "roots" that were valuable rather than shameful, it was one of the most significant changes to have occurred within black psychology. "Soul" music was important not just as a musical idiom, but also as a black-defined, black-accepted means of *actively* involving the mass base of Negroes. It was, in fact, the "self-definition" Stokely Carmichael was to call for later through cultural action rather than verbalized terms.

"Soul" music can also be seen as part of the secularization process. Claude Brown evokes the tone of the period vividly: " 'Soul' had started coming out of the churches and night-clubs into the streets. Everybody started talking about 'soul' as though it were something that they could see on people or a distinct characteristic of colored folks. . . . Everybody was really digging themselves, and thinking and saying in their behavior, in every action, 'Wow! Man, it's a beautiful thing to be colored.' Everybody was saying, 'Oh, the beauty of me!' "[13]

There was great speculation at the time as to the nature of "soul," whether or not and to what degree it was pecu-liarly the property of the Negro. It soon became evident that traditional analysis could not be used to define "soul," that "soul" was not subject to analysis at all. Ornette Cole-man offered an insight useful in drawing a distinction be-tween "soul" and "feeling": "Everybody feels. You know, even an animal feels; you hit him hard and he'll respond. But soul is another thing. And people get feeling all mixed up with soul, because undoubtedly soul must have something to do with being very natural and feeling must have some-thing to do with the choice of whether it hurt or didn't hurt or whether it made you happy or didn't make you happy. Choice that you can change. Soul must have something to do with where it's always positive and it's always com-plete."[14] "Soul," then, was related to the emotional involve-ment of oral orientation, "feeling" more closely related to the detached, intellectual process of categorization, i.e., one can ask *how* one feels. This posed an emotional center of black cultural experience, the cultural "where it's at," which was at peace with itself, "positive" and "complete." It was armed with the confidence of this new positive attitude that the black culture had emerged from its underground status in America to confront a white authority structure already beleaguered with negative and repressive infighting.

Only now being felt is the importance of the juxtaposition of the "soul" phenomenon and the new black positivism with a technocratic establishment culture visibly shaken by McCarthyism and swiftly retreating into cultural conservatism. It is partly a matter of not being able to see the forest for the trees; the events of the fifties, as they related to specific social issues, have only recently receded far enough into the past for broader cultural generalizations to be applied. I suggest, for example, that McCarthyism had the effect of forcing older liberals to regress to stability over specific, intellectualized issues and the simultaneous effect of radicalizing the youth, not over specific issues but, as a reaction to McCarthy's more general suppression of freedom of action, over the general quality of life in America. And, too, McCarthy's appeal to emotionalism caused an emotionalism of equal but opposite character in the young. Black music was particularly attractive because it could generate emotional release and because of its basic adherence to emotional truths: you cannot lie in the blues; during times of political crisis, truth for truth's sake is at a premium.

Black music was also the voice of the emerging "street culture." Within the predominantly white school structure which was under heavy attack from those who favored a purge of "leftist" thinking, it was becoming necessary for the more creative—certainly the more adventurous—students to seek educational experience outside the existing institutions, i.e., from black music. The family structure and the school structure were considered part of the same authority structure by the young. Abandoning either often meant abandoning both. Black music, then, brought the young out onto the streets.

In considering how and why black music became a voice of radical white Americans, it is also necessary to evaluate black music in terms of a pleasure principle. Even the most banal popular versions of "soul" material posed the rhetorical question, "What is wrong with feeling good?" Ray Charles's song "What'd I Say?" included calls that were sexually explicit—and had the effect of prohibiting this song, one of his huge successes, from being played on radio stations. Yet at no time was Charles's music lewd or obscene in terms of the contemporary standards. Its strength, rather, came from its *naturalness*. Black music during the fifties contributed to the basis of a life style that was a negation of Western analytic process—"soul" defied categorization —and that posited a near mystical naturalness, reaffirming biological priorities and denying the Puritan ethic of middle America. This opposition to established norms is at the heart of what Theodore Roszak recently called America's new "counter-culture," made up of radical whites separated from mainstream values by virtue of their youth.[15] Black culture, of course, has always been a "counter-culture."

The "soul" movement, unlike previous fashions in black music, seemed to affect Americans along age rather than class distinctions. The way various Americans applied this new black music indicates the nature of this generational rift. Older jazz critics, like Nat Hentoff, applied the music to their analysis of technocratic society in a somewhat detached manner. Hentoff wrote, "In an increasingly rationalized society, in which spontaneity and directness of emotion are constricted from kindergarten on to assure the maximum manipulative effectiveness of the directors of society, jazz had become one of the relatively few reservoirs of human warmth, human unpredictability, rawly human sounds, and faith in the perfectibility of man as controller of his own life."[16] The white "student as nigger," on the other hand, had assimilated black music at a more basic level—and during a more crucial stage—of his emotional development. Thus, Abbie Hoffman was to write in regard to the commercialization of "soul" music by white America, that "nothing else more than that rip-off of black music made me more ashamed of being white."[17] Hoffman and his contemporaries had so thoroughly identified with the music that they didn't have to try, like Hentoff, to intellectualize it; they had already accepted the oral orientation of nonanalysis and were learning how to apply the concept of actionality. Hoffman was to say further that "action is the only reality; not only reality but morality as well."[18] The anti-intellectualism and heightened emotionalism—indeed, the self-righteousness—of the young political activists in America during the sixties was thus predicated upon this kind of cultural activism during the fifties. Without the latter, there would have been no political activism at all, for it was upon a cultural basis of understanding that the earliest political coalitions, such as the Student Nonviolent Coordinating Committee in 1960, were formed. The cultural "left" in America thus antedated the political left. Allowing for differences in style, Hoffman's philosophy, or his antiphilosophy, of activism is not unlike that of Stokely Carmichael who was to say, ". . . don't worry about ideology. I always say that my work is my ideology. You will find that after you get going, your ideology will develop out of your struggle."[19] Significantly, Hoffman and Carmichael were contemporaries in the early days of SNCC activity in the South.

"Soul" music included that of both the black rhythm-and-blues players and the black jazz players. Ray Charles, the "high priest" of the rhythm-and-blues men, used the triplet feeling and the $\frac{6}{8}$ time of gospel music to great secular effect. Jazzmen were also developing this use of a three-against-four feeling, which maintained tension because the signature fraction could never be resolved into stasis. In fact, the basic approach of these two categories of black players was very similar, the main difference lying in the application of advanced technique by the jazzmen. Thus, this triplet tension emerged in the left-hand figures of jazz drummers, notably Elvin Jones, but with more subtlety and sophistication than it had in rhythm-and-blues music. In the jazz idiom, even before the "soul" phenomenon had gained wide currency, Charles Mingus was consciously working with the roots of black music to evolve a less intellectualized approach to jazz playing. It was based upon a thorough commitment to oral techniques in their capacity to promote emotional involvement, as opposed to intellectual detachment. Perhaps it was partly a reaction to "West Coast" jazz and partly a reflection of a prior need within black culture that Mingus's approach had such an enormous impact on all black players. Mingus preferred to sing parts to his musicians rather than write out even a basic chart of chord progressions, and many black musicians soon readopted this technique. In fact, when questioned about the chord progressions of one of his most lyrical solos with Mingus's group, alto saxophonist John Handy told me that he never actually knew the proper chords to the tune. In stressing total reliance on the "ears" of his musicians and in grooming drummer Dannie Richmond to play without depending on meter or bar line restrictions, Mingus established techniques that were viable for advanced jazz playing and yet still reminiscent of the earliest black music.

Another milestone group in the "soul" movement were the Jazz Messengers, led by Art Blakey in 1955. Their recording of *The Preacher* was the first out-and-out jazz record to be released as a single and sell over 100,000 copies. Horace Silver, the pianist of the group, although not a flashy player, became a major influence in contemporary jazz. Cecil Taylor, who developed into the most revolutionary black piano player and who had initially fallen under the influence of Dave Brubeck, recalls the effect Silver had on his music: "When I heard Horace, now that was a thing which turned me around and finally fixed my idea of piano playing. . . . Listening to Horace that night I dug that there were two attitudes in jazz, one white and one black. The white idea is valid in that the cats playing it play the way their environment leads them, which is the only way they can play. But Horace is the Negro idea because he was playing the real thing . . . with all the physicality of it."[20] Taylor's reaction was much like that of the early Southern players when they first heard Bolden play; in both cases, the oral orientation triumphed over the Western approach.

The Jazz Messengers, above all, stressed the ability to play the blues. They thus further stressed the advancement of techniques valid only in terms of the oral approach. The blues techniques developed by black jazz musicians often appeared unschooled, yet they were, in terms of good blues playing, superior techniques. As the black culture began to accept the validity of uniquely black solutions to problems of structure and content and as these solutions gained greater exposure, a combination of confidence and outrage— unparalleled in black American history—developed. It was on the basis of this new aggressiveness—as represented by the "soul" phenomenon—that many politically active Negroes gained the confidence to claim that integrationist trends in America, for example, were potentially misdirected. This idea was not new. Indeed, W. E. B. Du Bois had suggested as early as the first decade of the century that integration, in itself, was not an answer for the black culture if it meant surrendering its strength. Yet it was not until fifty years later that the masses of the black culture could, with good conscience, actively and vocally agree with him. By the sixties, however, Carmichael was to verbalize the sentiment that grew out of the "soul" phenomenon. "Integration," he said, "speaks to the problem of blackness in a despicable way. As a goal, it has been based on complete acceptance of the fact that in order to have a decent house or education, blacks must move into a white school. This reinforces among both black and white the idea that 'white' is automatically better and 'black' is by definition inferior."[21]

Cleaver has written that "prior to 1954, we [Negroes] lived in an atmosphere of Novocain. Negroes found it necessary, in order to maintain whatever sanity they could, to remain somewhat aloof and detached from 'the problem.' "[22] The "soul" movement was the catalyst that shocked the black culture out of this atmosphere of "Novocain." But, although it provided a cultural basis for much of the ensuing political revolution, it fast became a static and clichéd idiom of expression. Further, the "soul" movement had not been addressed to outsiders. It was part of a larger internal movement within black culture of self-definition. "If we do that," wrote Malcolm X, years later, "the whites will change their opinion automatically."[23] For all its clamor, the "soul" movement was, at bottom, not a *serious* challenge to Western conventions at all. Although it had had serious implications in terms of a challenge to the dominant Puritan ethic, the music itself was rarely more than party music. Jackie McLean, who worked with both Mingus and Blakey during the fifties, said as much: "Jazz is a party music; I know that when I play jazz, I'm always partying . . ."[24] In one sense, of course, this was its strength. In a larger sense, however, it was a sign of the ennui of the period: there was nothing else to do but party. It remained, then, for a more sophisticated, more *serious* approach to cultural confrontation tactics to elevate the black struggle to a position from which it could begin to verbalize, indeed, to recognize the very nature of its challenge to mainstream America.

Here, one is confronted with an interpretation of the motivations of the musicians of the period. It seemed clear from subsequent interviews that black musicians were extremely conscious of having to come up with a challenge of some proportion to American society and that the younger musicians were especially adamant on this point. These younger musicians, by and large, had learned their cultural stance through the information content of the bebop idiom and were gradually beginning to apply concrete terms of social analysis to clarify, albeit through hindsight, the social nature of that music. Interestingly enough, they were not attracted to issues such as integration versus segregation, so much as to more abstract—often even incomprehensible—generalizations about the nature of music as communication: how it could alter human behavior, how the musician's role in society, in general, indicated the suppression of a particular *kind* of truth. It was, in short, an examination by black musicians of the basic priorities of American society and a belief in music as an almost supernatural healing element. This, again, seems to reaffirm an extraordinary faith in, and hope for, the flexibility of American institutions. Perhaps history will show that it was in the sixties that the black lower class expressed faith in the nation's existing institutions for the last time.

Unlike "soul" music, the new "serious" music, developed by men like Miles Davis, John Coltrane, and Ornette Coleman, relied heavily on a thorough understanding of Western analysis, even if in time it was to reject that process as Coleman did. Davis and Coltrane became giants in the black culture specifically because they represented the elder statesmen, black men who had gone through the mill and survived, not empty-handed, but with peculiarly black solutions to peculiarly white problems. Their triumph and their acceptance by the black culture at a time when some of the jazz "avant-garde" were undergoing openly hostile treatment, lay in the fact that they had "paid their dues" in the old school and emerged with their individuality intact; they were the older, second generation bop musicians and, as such, had legitimized their claims to the leadership of the new. This "dues-paying" system is one way the oral culture maintains its continuity. Davis had worked with Parker, and Coltrane developed under Davis's wing. Thus, it was left to Coltrane and Davis to choose and groom the younger musicians who then themselves became recognized as "dues-paying" members of the black culture. At its best, this system provided a training ground for younger musicians. At its worst, it broke down into tight, personal cliques, especially in large cities where work was scarce, and encouraged infighting. To some extent, even infighting sharpened the tools of the young musician—a survival-of-the-fittest test in a culture that highly prized individuality of expression—and was therefore beneficial. Indeed, one of the most perplexing aspects of black music today—in the seventies—is that this "dues-paying" system is beginning to break down. The younger musicians appear to feel that there is not enough time left to go through normal channels, even within the black tradition. The dissolution of the "dues-paying" system indicates that the panic is on. Even though that system is a form of political patronage and limits an individual's chance to play (and makes music an "ass-kissing" business), it has also been a great source of continuity for the black culture. Its disappearance would be one symptom of the dissolution of the oral tradition as we know it.

Some musicians, however, stepped out of the stream of black tradition only to enrich it several years later. One, saxophonist Ornette Coleman, became a giant in the black culture almost by virtue of his isolation from it. It could perhaps be said that his isolation allowed him to get a true perspective on black culture and its relationship to white America, for, ultimately, Coleman became one of the more outspoken, articulate, and incisive social critics among contemporary black musicians. The reasons for his ostracism were ostensibly musical, yet they carried with them strong cultural implications. Bop had become highly stylized, and, especially after the "soul" movement, the ability to manipulate bop clichés became a major criterion of acceptance by the peer group of black musicians and by the black culture as well. Coleman knew how to play bop, as his first LP called *Something Else* attests. Here his group plays boppish tunes, and Coleman himself sounds suspiciously like an irrational version of Charles Parker. This "irrational" quality was, in fact, a manifestation of his early attempts to break free of the jazz clichés, much as Parker himself had through the use of "higher intervals." Unlike Parker, who advanced through innovations in the harmonic aspect of jazz, a tradition continued by both Davis and Coltrane, Coleman was striving to dispense with the Western segment of jazz playing: he was striving to play *without regard* to harmony. He was ostracized by the majority of black musicians because his innovations were too radical for the times. They felt Coleman did not know how to play his horn because it sounded as if he rarely played to the same musical idea twice. In fact, his conception, which he called "free group improvisation," was similar to what Herskovitz had called "the deification of accident" within African culture. "When our group plays," said Coleman, "before we start out to play, we do not have any idea what the end result will be. Each player is free to contribute what he feels in the music at any given moment. We do not begin with a preconceived notion as to what kind of effect we will achieve."[25]

Coleman insisted on the melody growing out of the vocalized *approach* to melody playing. "There are some intervals that carry that *human* quality if you play them in the right pitch. I don't care how many intervals a person can play on an instrument; you can always reach into the human sound of a voice on your horn if you're actually hearing and trying to express the warmth of the human voice."[26] Further, this vocalized approach was part of the individual fitting into primitive patterns of nature. This was also a reaction against the more repetitive aspects of "soul" and "hard bop" rhythm section work; Coleman suggested that "rhythm patterns should be more or less like natural breathing patterns. I would like the rhythm section to be as free as I'm trying to get."[27] Coleman was basically an innovator who created shortcuts through the body of oral tradition to arrive at conclusions similar to those derived by more conventional players, through more conventional means, years later. Ultimately, the younger Coleman's music had a profound effect on even the most mature black jazzmen. Perhaps his most revolutionary effort, a record called *Free-Jazz*, best represents this influence. In this record, he achieved a kind of collective freedom that even John Coltrane (re: *Ascension*) would try to achieve years later, and his intensely spirited approach to music foreshadowed the "energy" players of the late sixties. These players, like Albert Ayler and Archie Shepp, wore the label because of the incredible dynamics of their music. Whereas Mingus and the soul players had shouted, the post-Coleman, post-Coltrane players screamed. Recalling the impact of Buddy Bolden's "loud" or "rough" style during the early years of the century, wherein sheer decibel level was used to produce a music that was frankly rude in the face of social conventions (i.e., a "new way" of playing), both *Free-Jazz* and *Ascension* radically altered the direction of jazz playing and the limits of accepted experimentation. The formal structure of music was reduced to the most basic common denominator of black musical tradition: the striving for personal freedom through complete collective catharsis.

In their search for new sources of structure and information, black musicians began to disregard Western forms as a matter of course. This move was predicated, in part, upon the pioneering model approach of the Miles Davis sextet during 1958. Davis's approach worked, in practice, a good deal like early blues technique. The tunes were composed of few chords, all of which were in such a relation to a dominant tone row—or mode—as to allow the soloist to continue improvising along a kind of blues scale, without regard to the actual modulation of the chords, bar by bar. The result was that the soloist was given more room to improvise, more harmonic "space" in which to move, and the *tension* of any given piece was not broken into 12-, 16-, 14-, or 32-bar fragments, even though the tunes were constructed along these standard divisions. This opened up a new kind of long form improvisation that could apply to any popular song. Davis said of this approach, as best heard on his *Kind of Blue* record: "When you go this way, you can go on forever. You don't have to worry about changes (chord progressions), and you can do more with the line. It becomes a challenge to see how melodically inventive you are. When you're based on chords, you know at the end of 32 bars that the chords have run out and there's nothing to do but repeat what you've just done."[28] Davis's innovations thus helped free all musicians from the repetition of bop playing and added a new emphasis on the melodic aspect of playing, that aspect which best represents the *individual's* voice. They also paved the way for the final assault on Western song forms that were to be carried out by Coltrane.

Coltrane, who was a member of this quintet, used Davis's modal frameworks to carry harmonic improvisation to its ultimate extension, playing as many notes and scales as rapidly as he could. After Coltrane had finished playing a sequence of chords, it seemed there was nothing left to say, nothing new to build on those progressions. Subsequently, many black players stopped relying on the Western song forms for a basis of improvisation. There was a feeling of "doom" about Coltrane's playing, particularly after his record *Giant Steps* was released. Many listeners felt that he was consciously trying to play the old forms into the ground, to destroy them from within. Because he played so many notes so fast, he "had to put the notes in uneven groups like fives and sevens in order to get them all in."[29] Like the ¾ time feeling, the ⁵⁄₄ and ⁷⁄₄ time feeling Coltrane generated by placing groups of 5 or 7 notes against the 4 beats carried by the rhythm section created a new kind of tension that did not resolve at the end of bars or in expected places. This in turn created new anticipations in the listener, and musicians began likening this new feeling to "freedom," the word most often used by musicians to describe Coltrane's music, or indeed that of any of the post-Coltrane, post-Coleman musicians. One must also mention the brief few months Coltrane put in with Thelonious Monk's quintet at the Five Spot Cafe. Monk, who once broke up Charlie Parker with a single, well-placed note from the piano after innumerable bars of utter silence, is the master of redistributing the rhythmic feel of a piece. Also in the group was bassist Wilbur Ware who superimposed chord substitutions, building the tension so that when he came back to the basics of the tune, it felt "like everything sucked in." Monk's music, Coltrane had said, is "just like simple truths." By the time Coltrane formed his own quartet (McCoy Tyner, Elvin Jones, and Jimmy Garrison), he was well on the way to the synthesis of harmonic simplicity and harmonic complexity which made his music a vortex of screams and simple songs. It was in the early sixties that critics, particularly in *Down Beat* magazine, started labeling his music *angry, anti* or *free* jazz.

In relating black musical expression to the liberation of black social aggression, it is useful to consider Lorenz's approach, which recognizes, first, that aggression is a normal and inherent part of the human personality and, second, that if it does not find an outlet in "ritualization," it will dissipate itself through physical violence. Black music is a kind of "ritualization," or imitation of nature, which can channel black aggression toward constructive and creative ends. It does not drain away that aggression but redirects it, in a more highly articulated form, back through the black community. It does not divert social aggression so much as it uses aggression as a tool to reeducate the individual whose initial orientations it seeks to alter. During the late fifties,

black musicians began consciously using music toward this
end at the same time that they began throwing off the yoke
of heroin. The result was a highly spiritual social philosophy
based on the potential of black music to alter social orientations and value structures. Like Coleman, who developed
along with his musical innovations an elaborate conception of
"social love," Coltrane could attribute his musical development, in part, to his "spiritual awakening." In a period of
less than a year, he had kicked his heroin habit and become
involved with music as "an instrument which can create the
initial thought patterns that can change the thinking of
people."[30] Malcolm X was to say several years later that
"once you change your thought pattern, you change your
attitude. Once you change your attitude, it changes your behavior pattern and then you go into some action."[31] Coltrane,
then, was not an "angry" man but, rather, a visionary in the
communications revolution.

Whereas heroin had been functional as an emotionally
repressive device during the "wait-and-see" phase of the
early fifties, it became a social liability when the cultural
conflict moved into an actional phase. Heroin use in jazz
playing declined at the same time that aggression was boil-
ing over within black communities throughout the United
States. As early as 1956, Robert Williams led a chapter of
the NAACP which began arming itself in "self-defense."
Williams wrote that "we grasped the relationship between
violence and racism. The Afro-American is a 'militant' because he defends himself, his family, his home, and his dignity."[32] The earliest black aggression, then, was used *de-
fensively* against American violence and racism. It is perhaps
important to suggest that whereas Williams, like the Black
Panthers after him, was basically engaged in this defensive
action, the musicians sought to alter the "initial thought
patterns" of black Americans, and were, in fact, engaged in
more primary, more direct, and more assertive tactics.

Coltrane's music, which was his social philosophy in action, had been gradually moving away from Western forms well before he discovered Indian music and Eastern philosophy. Yet these Eastern influences became important to him if only because, as he indicated, they were a source of education outside the Western tradition. The social function of Eastern philosophies turned out to be as important as the non-Western forms found in Eastern music. Eastern philosophies are spiritual postures with direct secular application, the kind of secular spirituality toward which black culture had been moving, through music, for years. Further, Oriental religions endow their gods with *human* faculties, which may have appealed to the American Negroes' demand for justice in the *here* and *now*. Finally, Eastern philosophies are centered on absolute *resistance*, like the existential *no*, to the currents of world affairs. As Stokely Carmichael stressed, the black man's first problem was getting over the fear of saying *no* to white value structures. The appeal of Indian music was based also on its role in society: it is neither "Art" music in the Western sense nor "popular" music but, rather, "exalted folk" music. Whereas the bop musicians had sought entry into the world of Western Art, Coltrane and his contemporaries forced blacks and whites alike finally to confront the role of Art in society and to reassess Western value structures. This was no subtle assault on the aesthetic sensibilities of his audience; one of the drummers who worked with Coltrane during the last years of his life told me: "We are getting to the point where we can make the audience laugh or cry or scream, or just do anything. We're getting ready to leap off and wake these people up. We're taking them with us."

The increasing cathartic power of this new music, called "avant-garde," "new thing," or "new wave" jazz, was a function of the growing necessity for violent catharsis within the black community. This can be related, in part, to urban pressures and to the amplification of social energy in a highly compressed body of people. In part, it can be related back to the very nature of the new music itself, inasmuch as the music of Coltrane and a handful of others actually had the effect of psychologically liberating people. Many people, black and white, have attested to the therapeutic value of this new music. One black musician told me he stopped formal psychotherapy sessions after hearing Coltrane's group in person, and one psychiatrist upon hearing Coltrane's *Kulu Se Mama* started using the record in his work. He said of Coltrane, "It's fantastic! It sounds like a man strapped down and finally screaming to be free." The extended improvisation of the Coltrane quartet left both audience and musicians physically and emotionally spent, yet spiritually strong. It became a confrontation music of the most basic type: it challenged the individual, at the fundamental level of perception, to put down his prejudices and preconceptions and allow himself to be an intuitive animal. At bottom, Coltrane's music, like Monk's music and like the blues itself, was built on empirical, "simple truths." What distinguished the new music from what had come before it was its incredible dynamism: the new musicians *would* be heard. There was no way to be exposed to it and remain indifferent.

Within the community of black musicians, the confrontation rapidly spread to include a direct challenge to the very economics of the music business. Several black musicians, like Andrew Hill, have suggested that this was part of their initial intention, yet I suspect that it was a secondary reaction to the nightclub atmosphere and that it grew out of the very nature of the new music. The fact that most club owners are white tended to extend the black musician's attack to the white culture in general. One of Cecil Taylor's bass players articulated the connection between the anti-capitalist nature of black music and the subsequent attack on Western capitalism: "Trying to make a living with Cecil is absolutely unbelievable," he said, "because there is no economic advantage to playing like that. It's completely unsalable in the nightclubs because of the fact that each composition lasts, or could last, an hour and a half. Bar owners aren't interested in this, because if there is one thing they hate to see, it's a bunch of people sitting around open-mouthed with their brains absolutely paralyzed by the music, unable to call for the waiter."[33] The new music was moving toward creating an immediate and substantial response in the audience. No longer was it a casual party, or background, music. Taylor himself, reacting to the economic nature of his music, proposed that "there should be a boycott by Negro musicians of all jazz clubs in the United States. I also propose that there should be a boycott by Negro jazz musicians of all record companies. I also propose that all Negro jazz musicians boycott all trade papers and journals dealing with music. And I also propose that all Negro musicians resign from every federated union in this country that has anything to do with music. . . . We're no longer reflecting or vibrating to the white-energy principle. The point is: we know who we are. We have a whole history of music in this country."[34] Two points emerge out of Taylor's statement, even though, in fact, not even he followed the above advice. First, black self-consciousness had become so intense as to come into conflict with the institutions upon which black music, itself, was built. Indeed, Ornette Coleman stopped playing in nightclubs because none could meet his price; his reason, he said, was that he knew the "true worth" of his music. Second, black musicians had discovered "who they were," not through any body of literature on the subject, but through the whole history of black music in America. During a time when, as we shall see, many white youths were struggling to disassociate themselves from their elders, the more militant black youth was gaining strength from theirs. The significant aspect of the process was that they had begun to recognize the validity of the oral tradition, whether or not they conceived of it as such. Again, black music does not operate at the level of opinions but, rather, alters perception and the nature of perceptual information.

The new music thus became a confrontation music. Those who preferred it were clearly aligned with the black "cause"; in fact, merely enjoying it implied espousing the black cause. This, then, was one of the central reasons why it was taken up so readily by liberal white youths on major college campuses. Many of these youths had returned from summer projects in the South to aid voter registration, and those who hadn't worked for civil rights found in the acceptance of black music a kind of spiritual substitute for political involvement. The middle sixties began an era of cultural polarization caused by the black issue. The black leaders of SNCC had told white workers that they were no longer needed or wanted in the South, that they should return to their own white "ghettos" to organize against the sources of racism. Thus began the war on the rich, as opposed to the war on poverty. It seemed there was no black "problem," there was only a near congenital "white problem." In 1966, Carmichael had picked up Adam Clayton Powell's expression *Black Power* and, using it now as a tool to drive white support back to the North, stressed the need for blacks to organize around the fact of their blackness. Whites, driven from the political arena of the South, were more than ever thrown back upon those cultural foundations that supported their alliance with the black cause. An informal survey conducted for a major record distributor on college campuses during the winter of 1966–67 showed that, first, middle-class whites were purchasing increasing quantities of "hard core" black music, whether it was the sophisticated jazz of Coltrane or the blues of Muddy Waters or James Brown and, second, that there was a direct relationship between the interest in these records and an antiestablishment cultural orientation.[35] The students were purchasing these records partly as a source of information as to the nature of the black revolution and partly as a means of aligning themselves with that revolution. Many young black musicians who were not yet accepted by the black culture, such as Marion Brown, Albert Ayler, and Roscoe Mitchell, were promptly canonized by white youth. Indeed, Archie Shepp sold more records on college campuses in the North than he did in the black communities, a fact that in 1968 he admitted displeased him.

And yet, a major reason for the extraordinary popularity of black music on college campuses was its apolitical nature. A distinction must be made between the cultural revolution and the political revolution, as represented by the civil rights activists on the one hand and the early "street people" on the other. As late as the middle sixties, fraternity and sorority organizations carried on a form of parentally approved supervision of young whites on campus. Yet, as I have suggested, as early as the days of the McCarthy "witch hunts," many of the more creative students had assumed the role of social outcasts—that is, they left home, if only spiritually— in order to sever ties with the establishment authority structure, represented by both the family unit and the school system. Jeff Nuttall traces this rift in the generations further back, to the atomic bomb, claiming that with the atomic age came the beginning of "life without a future" for the young. He has written, "The people who had not yet reached puberty at the time of the bomb were incapable of conceiving of life *with* a future. They might not have had any direct preoccupation with the bomb. This depended largely on their sophistication. But they never knew a sense of future . . . Dad was a liar . . . He lied about the bomb and he lied about the future . . . The so-called 'generation gap' started then and has been increasing ever since."[36] When these students arrived on campus, they were at first labeled *independents* as a means of distinguishing them from the hypothetical norm, which included any *organized* activity —the fraternities as well as the civil rights movement. This *independent* label was deceptive inasmuch as it belied the fact that these students were reaching out for new forms of social collectivity, apart from, even aside from, the tradition of even the most radical political organizations. These spiritually homeless, or unaffiliated, students ultimately came to constitute the hard core of the "street culture," as it developed simultaneously at Berkeley, California, Madison, Wisconsin, and Cambridge, Massachusetts. Because their initial common denominator was their disaffiliation from the norm as well as their distrust for any organized movement, regardless of how "radical" the intent, they tended to adopt for social archetypes people who were not motivated by "acceptable" social behavior. The "bad nigger" became the hero of the North. Malcolm X was all right because he had gone to prison. John Coltrane was even better because one needn't relate to the very literary bias of Western life to participate in his genius. Black music and its derivatives, then, provided a basis for collectivity for students who were not only "social misfits" but "cultural misfits" as well. "Woodstock Nation," then, was both a mirror image of the conformist norm as well as an experiment in its dissolution.

As I have stressed, the real strength behind the oral culture in America, its continuity lay in the fact that it remained "popular" culture. Often, the jazz musicians were forced to cut themselves off from the mass base in order to move the music forward. Rhythm-and-blues musicians, while more hesitant to do this, were also becoming more willing to introduce advanced elements into their music. Thus, although jazz music tends to move toward exclusivity and rhythm-and-blues often goes through periods of banality, black music in general has gravitated toward the consensus of contemporary black taste. American whites have had to enter the stream of black music as best they could. Those who were not prepared for the sophistication of jazz were generally exposed to the same basic elements through their interest in black rhythm-and-blues. Although an interest in the Rolling Stones or the Beatles was not even second best to exposure to Sonny Boy Williamson, Bo Diddley or B. B. King, the fact that these British musicians had publicly acknowledged their debt to black bluesmen tended to lead even the least adventurous whites to the source of today's popular music. Thus, often inadvertently, black taste has dictated white taste in popular music for more than a decade. It should be stressed that James Brown's screams and the two drummers he employed to generate an enormous rhythmic dynamism were more revolutionary than were his somewhat controversial lyrics, which included "I'm Black and I'm Proud" and "Don't want nobody to give me nothing, open the door, I'll get it myself," *especially* because they were not *recognized* as being revolutionary. The techniques of the oral culture thus met with little opposition and altered the perception, and so the behavior, of young Americans in the privacy of their own homes.

The establishment had begun lamenting the moral decay and spiritual apathy of the younger generation as early as the fifties. What has today become evident is that the younger generation is, in fact, a highly spiritual group. What continues to disconcert the establishment is that this spirituality is not of the Western tradition, nor does it conform to any preconceived notions of "rational" spiritual behavior. It is easy for them to pass off the overt occultism and the popularized interest in astrology as "faddish." But it is perhaps next to impossible for middle-aged, middle-class whites to consider that when John Coltrane was playing, *he was praying* (his music *was* his ideology); or that when James Brown sang about feeling "like a sex machine," he also conjured up spirits that have nothing to do with either sex or "rational" behavior but which, nonetheless, motivate people toward freedom. Coltrane's stress on inner strength, verbalized on the liner notes of his *Love Supreme* album, was elaborated by young black musicians into a complex theory of "energy" playing. Coltrane had hired Pharoah Sanders as a sideman in the late sixties because, as he said at the time, "Pharoah is very strong in spirit and will, and these are the things that I like to have up there . . . I like to have this energy."[37] After Coltrane's death, in the summer of 1967, Sanders became a leader in the "new wave" of jazz, largely because of his spiritual posture. A member of Sanders's group described him as "having a halo" when he played, and the music created an "energy field" that made the drummer feel he was hovering "six inches off the floor."

One can find in this rhetoric a human application of modern, technological jargon. Yet the notion of "inner strength" is more than just verbal glibness. It was "inner strength," for example, that attracted many thousands of Negroes to the Black Muslim movement. The downfall of the racist doctrines of the Muslims through Malcolm X's enlightenment in Mecca served to prove that "inner strength" is closely associated with an antiracist humanism. Malcolm's message from Mecca had said, "I no longer subscribe to sweeping indictments of one race. . . . In all honesty and sincerity it can be stated that I wish nothing but freedom . . . for all people."[38] This spirit of universal brotherhood and multiracial freedom was a major tenet of the new black music. The Black Panther party which ultimately split with Carmichael over the issue of racism, as Malcolm had done with the Muslims, also used the "inner strength" doctrine to combat heroin addiction within the ghetto, several years after the vanguard of musicians had initiated the campaign.[39] "Inner strength" can thus be associated with the individual's ability to transcend behavior imposed by mass action: what Malcolm and the Panthers were verbalizing, black musicians had been achieving through their playing and through interaction with their audience. Black music, then, was the experiment that proved the theory several years before the theory had even been articulated. Within the white culture there had also been a great deal of interest in the notion of "inner strength"; however it was qualitatively different both in its conception and application from that of the black culture. The difference between the Beatles' infatuation with the Maharishi and the spiritual content of Coltrane's music was as enormous as, let's say, the difference between the *verbal* glibness of a young man cut off from his culture and the *physical* dedication of a mature man who is very much a part of his. It is not superficial that the white "counter-culture" has had to rely so strongly on black culture for its spiritual direction, for it has been only through this contact that young whites have been able to find the physical application of spirituality operating on a mass, or popular, level.

Interestingly enough, a recent fund-raising drive by the Panthers in New York, a three-day, continuous music festival, included practically all the contemporary black jazz players but only a few of the contemporary black rhythm-and-blues musicians. This may be an indication that the black masses are achieving a level of sophistication equal to that of the black jazzman of several years ago and hence that the "new thing" is more acceptable. At the same time, it can be pointed out that many of the black rhythm-and-blues artists, because of their commercial orientation and success within the white world, are now considered too "liberal." There is also a countertrend to this situation, which finds some black rhythm-and-blues men joining with black jazz musicians to form a new kind of modern cultural synthesis, the contemporary version of early Kansas City blues or the jazz/ soul band of Ray Charles during the early fifties. In 1969, for example, B. B. King recorded with Pharoah Sanders.

Finally, it should be clear that black taste in music is becoming more "serious"—i.e., "avant-garde" jazz is becoming more palatable to even the least sophisticated Negro—because the "party" is becoming more serious. One need look only as far as the fact that during 1968–69 there were twenty-nine Black Panthers killed by police across the country to guess at just how serious the popular culture of black America has become.

Both the "party" nature of black music and its "serious" social intentions have maintained working relationships with, and established a kind of cultural common ground for, radical elements in America. The most influential multiracial pop group of the moment, Sly and the Family Stone, has been hailed as one of the best musical groups in America by Miles Davis, whose own recent releases, *In a Silent Way* through *Live at the Fillmore,* suggest a strong "pop" influence. The real antiestablishment nature of the new black/white alliance did not come out on an elevated plane of discussion; yet the metaphysical jargon was appealing to white youths who had "discovered" hallucinogenic drugs, just as the political drift of Archie Shepp who said, "We see jazz as . . . antiwar; it is opposed to Vietnam; it is for Cuba; it is for the liberation of all people"[40] was appealing to white youths who sought an alliance between leftist groups, such as SDS and the black community. Rather, it was the music *as* ideology that reflected the true nature of the alliance. As one black musician told me: "See, here's what's happening. See, blacks didn't know that they were . . . that they were enslaved and that they weren't free. They didn't know that until not too long ago. [This reference coincides with Cleaver's notion of an "atmosphere of Novocain" prior to 1954.] And then when all the younger white kids found out that *they* weren't free, them motherfuckers said that they were gonna change this shit. That's right. That's what's happening today. We're finding out that *all* of us are not free. It's just got different degrees, you know?" Hence, the "free group improvisation" of Coleman, the long form improvisation and rhythmic intensity of Coltrane, and even the dynamism of James Brown's band provided a perceptual orientation that allowed whites and blacks alike to break out of old thought patterns and, occasionally, to reexamine the limitations of their personal freedom in terms of *cultural* suppression.

This filtering of an alternative life style into the white middle-class community caused considerable turmoil within the white establishment culture. One recent Harris poll, for example, showed that "college demonstrators" were more generally detested by middle-Americans than prostitutes, atheists, and homosexuals; while another poll showed that middle-Americans considered the "youth problem" more urgent than the Vietnam war and the issue of economic inflation.[41] One can doubt the veracity of these findings, of course, but one cannot ignore the central issue that caused the pollsters to ask these kinds of questions to begin with. This fear on the part of the establishment culture indicates that the challenge to Western institutions based on an oral orientation is not superficial. There are, naturally, political aspects to consider, with Negroes now controlling an increasing number of urban centers, in terms of population if not immediate political power, and with the franchise being extended to eighteen-year-olds. The real issue, however, is not whether this counter-culture will choose to alter American institutions through politics or through violence because in either case it would be Western institutions whose basic legitimacy was being recognized. In this sense, even the more militant political organizations like the Black Panthers are still "keeping the faith" in American society the black man has traditionally shown. The real danger lies not in the violence of a culture with roots in spontaneous, collective modes of actionality, but in something, in Silberman's phrase, "deeper and far more corrosive; a sense of permanent alienation from American society."[42]

The modern American revolutionary struggles against a society that doesn't understand him, against the deaf ear mainstream America has always turned to the oral culture. And the lack of comprehension on the part of mainstream culture serves only to legitimize the revolutionary's alienation and scorn. However, in times of ultimate crisis, the white radical can always return to the fold, but the Negro, kept apart by a basic color caste system, must remain outside. Further, there is a built-in frustration in the situation of the radical black, for on the one hand, he claims that the prefix *Negro* is "dehumanizing," that there is something unnatural in being classified by race, while on the other hand, he feels that integration is less acceptable than segregation in contemporary America. This alienation from mainstream culture, then, remains basically a circular and unresolvable problem peculiar to the Negro.

Increased technology in the urban environment has brought wealth to white America and growing unemployment to black America. Negroes are an economic as well as a racial, or cultural, minority. The process of acculturation does not seem to "take" with the black culture, partly because Negroes have not been moving up the socioeconomic ladder on a par with whites. Sixty years ago, Du Bois recognized the reasons for this as twofold; first, the Negro's cultural orientation is at odds with capitalism: "[he has] a disdain for mere cash. He'll loaf before your face and work behind your back." Yet Du Bois also saw that this opposition to capitalism was, to a certain extent, the result of a failure on the part of American society: "They [Negroes] are careless because they have not found that it pays to be careful; they are improvident because the improvident ones of their acquaintance get on about as well as the provident."[43] Hence, the level of disaffection and bitterness within the black community has been steadily rising with the process of urbanization itself. Current unemployment among blacks is as much as four times as great as that for whites, a substantial proportionate increase on the average figures for the past decade. Along with the bitterness of this growing disparity comes a loss of faith in the flexibility of American institutions. The real danger, then, comes when the Negro, acting out of despair, *ceases to care.*

Although one should not underestimate the ability of American society to absorb dissent and to buy time for spiritual crises with material placebos, one should not minimize the disheartening effect of economic disparity joined to overt, hard-line repression. The situation has become critical. As one black minister, who along with many others has been radicalized since the Nixon administration's "law and order" crackdown said: "I've never seen repression come down like this in my life. . . . You can kill a nigger any time you want. But we're not going to stand for it any more; we're going to start taking people with us."[44] One black musician used more vivid "street" vocabulary to say essentially the same thing: "This is Fat City protest. What you got is a lot of soulful kamikazes who don't care if they die, you dig it? These brothers are doing it to *end* it." And yet, as we have seen, external enmity has traditionally been used by the black culture to consolidate its position. It has, in fact, been a major factor in the coherency of the oral tradition and, as such, has had a positive effect on the development of alternatives to mainstream American values. Thus, the insidious effects of America's economic policies are perhaps more crucial to modern black alienation than are the overt signs of cultural warfare. The welfare system, for example, attacks the symptoms of modern social problems in such a way as to make the disease more serious. Welfare is entirely *ma-*

terially oriented. One cannot cure boredom or spiritual disaffection this way.

The growing response of black musicians to economic criteria of success rather than to the aesthetic criteria of the oral tradition is certainly a sign of the contemporary black disaffection. The example of the exceptionally talented black musician who could not earn even a substandard living in New York City best sums up the new fatalism. When I spoke with him, he was sitting in his small room in uptown New York: "Just waiting for the revolution to move down to Fifth Avenue." He said, "It doesn't make a man any greater being able to play and all that, and being an artist and all that. Tell that shit to the rent man, you know, tell that to a doctor or something, you know, he don't give a *damn* who you are . . . he wants to know what color your money is . . . he don't even care what color you are. He'll even accept you if you got some money. But it doesn't matter if you have soul or not, or if you have this or if you have that, you know, it's back to money. It's just an outside thing anyway. Can't nobody feel what I feel inside. That's why none of that shit doesn't matter." I asked him if he did not feel that John Coltrane, who owned an expensive house and car at the time of his death, had made a good living from music; he answered that Coltrane made "some chump change," but only because "he remained faithful and true to *the thing,* and I ain't got that long you know, because *this* is not life at all, not this part."

The unanswerable question about the relationship of black music to a black oral continuum hangs on whether or not the oral culture is beginning to break up under the pressures of an urban, technocratic society that finds the oral orientation more of an economic and social disadvantage than ever before. The Negro's bitterness and loss of hope was evident in the very secularization process brought on by urban development: The Negro turned away from the church partly because he didn't want to "feel *too* much." Today, among young urban Negroes, suicide has become a serious problem; it is twice as frequent among New York Negroes between twenty and thirty-five, for example, as among whites of the same age.[45] Any forecast of the future nature and role of the oral culture in America must be made with an eye on the historical precedents, and for these one can look to the history of black music. Its development and the development of the oral culture in general have been dependent upon two facets of the oral orientation: the strength of collective improvisation and the importance of the individual innovator. The historical trend has shown that innovation was based on collective group actionality in the early days but that with urbanization, it gradually shifted to the point where the individual innovator dominated the group. Even the return to collective improvisation, which had become a major trend during the sixties, depended upon the innovations of a few dominant individuals. If economic pressures do not completely stifle individual initiative and if cultural repression does not kill off what remains (that is, if the creative genius that the oral culture has traditionally spawned is not withered in its seed by an increasingly hostile environment), then the oral culture will continue to thrive and to give meaning to even the most "senseless" violence.

The evidence is not altogether promising. Through the years, music has been the major survival tactic for black America. The music from Bolden through Coltrane has been used as a primary source of information and as instruction in how best to apply that information. As one young Negro said about the death of Coltrane, "We have lost a great leader. Trane [Coltrane]—more than anyone else except maybe Malcolm—showed the younger generation how to stand up and be proud of themselves." One symptom of the breakup of the oral continuum is that there has been no really new musical innovation since the early sixties, and even the innovations of the late fifties and early sixties were done, with few exceptions, by musicians over the age of thirty-five. Even Coleman's ideas had been tried by other musicians during the forties, but Parker had so thoroughly dominated the scene that they were written off. Another, more disconcerting symptom is that there appear to be fewer young black musicians entering the music profession. The recorded evidence seems to substantiate this lack of young talent in great numbers. Since the early sixties, a handful of established players have reappeared on records, with only occasional additions. One reason may be that jazz has become extraordinarily difficult to master, technically, and so fewer nineteen-year-old "prodigies" are to be found.

The depth and effect of this breakup are difficult to assess. I would suggest only the most general kind of theory: the confrontation music which grew out of the bebop idiom changed the articulated relationship of black and white Americans. Prior to the forties, black music itself was more or less the articulated statement of the oral culture. Since the forties, however, black musicians have grown increasingly verbal in their defense of the black culture. This has brought on what I have called the new visibility of black culture in American media, seen, at its extreme, in the picture of Thelonious Monk on the cover of *Time*. Monk became news twenty years too late. This new visibility has had two major effects. First, in the tradition of Western literacy: to define a thing is to dispense with it. The black position has become somewhat less tenable ever since it has become articulated through linear semantics. The strength of the oral tradition was undermined by the rules of Western literacy. Second, the new visibility has allowed the American establishment to focus on the source of black disaffection and to handle it with *repressive tolerance*. Previously, only random symptoms of black disaffection had come to the surface and were either ignored or summarily dealt with by the Western tradition. However, once it had become clear that the real issue was not piecemeal gains but the restructuring of American society, the cultural establishment gained an advantage. They were then able to placate the black musician (i.e., to "tolerate" him) and to draw the oral culture into the political arena. This rechanneled its energy into programs aimed at checking revolutionary social change. Many potential young black musicians are now black "activists"—in the political sense—and may be faced with either winning their immediate objectives, and thus losing their freedom, or with losing their lives.

And yet, there is cause to believe that the oral tradition will continue. It can be suggested, for example, that increased white repression will create an even greater demand for a nonverbal channel of communication within both black and white America and that the social nature of black music may become even more significant to the future of American society. White radicals have already begun to operate in small collectives, or "affinity groups," whether for the purposes of isolation from mainstream America, as in the communes, or those of urban warfare. These small collectives are providing a somewhat viable base for the integration of the individual into the operation of social events. In this sense, as spontaneous collectivity becomes a necessity of modern life, the survival tactics of the oral orientation may become more widespread. The specific role of black music in this process, like its role throughout American history, is more easily felt than explained. I would suggest, for example, that the ability of black music to generate an extended family has been applied. The interest in black music among almost all young people today—and not just a passing interest but an intense identification—is the natural tendency of youth to gravitate toward where the warmth and the light and the heat are. White affinity groups are known by their members as "families"; black music is one of the strongest bonds in this new family structure.

It should be noted, also, that young people need to give respect—to have some life held up to them as a model—as much as they need to receive it. Black musicians have pioneered in a contemporary masculinity, and they have remained true to a source of higher values. As such, they have become models for a twentieth-century "natural man." Their music has flowed from the belief that the individual can free himself through collective action of the most intuitive sort, and they themselves have both the mobility and the element of surprise so highly prized in twentieth-century America. If Western man has "lost" his masculinity to the machines and corporate structures he lives to serve, the black musician, whose work is his play and whose orientation is the polar opposite of technological, increases his importance as a social archetype. He will, therefore, continue to create the "initial thought patterns" of a great many people.

Whether or not the oral tradition will continue *as we know it* is impossible to guess. I have attempted to sketch its history and give the odds. I suspect that neither the dissolution of the "dues-paying system" nor the occurrence of "repressive tolerance" is taking place at so rapid a rate as to jeopardize the oral continuum. In social terms, perhaps Charles Hamilton said it well enough: "The victim of continued social oppression brings to the situation a wholly different set of views of what is legitimate for change. The victim is more willing—much more willing—to risk the future because he has very little to lose and a lot to gain. . . . We cannot emphasize too much this relatively simple idea: that the two groups operate from different vantage points and different concepts of what constitutes legitimacy."[46] Inasmuch as black music is a tool for social change, regardless of whether it is regarded as such by either the victim or the oppressor, there is no reason to believe that it will not continue to be used to best advantage by all who come in contact with it.

And yet, as I have stressed, the revolutionary nature of the music itself—its influence in the raw, perceptual sphere —is perhaps more important than its overt social function. It is a way of seeing things and a manner of projecting that vision. When the musician plays, he is objectifying his experience, and, further, playing it for others makes everybody feel better because there is great solace in the experience of community. Music is thus a great force for unity and peace today. The fear that wild music could drive people "mad" was based on the stereotypical image of black culture conjured up by Western man. First, Western man invented this notion of "madness," and then chose to become afraid of it. It appears to be the case, however, that even wild music can help to keep people sane, inasmuch as sanity must have something to do with feeling "positive and complete" or "at one" with oneself. I think it is very significant that those people who have come to rely on the sort of music I have characterized as "oral" have also come to judge the straight world as *actually* insane. The pigeon has come home to roost. And thus music is also a great cause of contention today. As long as the culture in power treats black music and its derivatives as "shallow," black musicians and their derivatives will continue to move deeper underground, in spirit, even as their acceptance is more universal. Perhaps it is not altogether irrelevant to suggest that a subculture emotionally and culturally entrenched is not one that can be coerced by violence—or even blatant injustice—nor one that is willing to retreat very far. This is not a new crisis but a very old one which is gathering quickly. In the circumlocutory style of one last anonymous musician: "The vast majority of Americans never have had any musical taste. I mean, just dig the national anthem. And that anthem—

which nine out of ten Americans cannot even sing because the release is out of the range of the normal human voice—that anthem was chosen by Congress fairly recently when really good tunes, the 'Battle Hymn of the Republic' to name only one, were available. And a country's anthem has a lot to do with it because you'll find that, especially today, a lot of people haven't been singing along."

APPENDICES

NOTES

INTRODUCTION

1. Julius Lester, *Look Out, Whitey! Black Power's Gon' Get Your Mama!* p. 90.

2. Raymond Williams, *The Long Revolution,* pp. 66, 67–69.

1. ORAL CULTURE AND MUSICAL TRADITION

1. C.D. Broad, quoted in Aldous Huxley, *The Doors of Perception,* p. 22.

2. Colin Cherry, *On Human Communication,* p. 125.

3. Marshall McLuhan, *Understanding Media,* p. 82.

4. Claude Lévi-Strauss, *The Savage Mind,* p. 15.

5. Arthur Koestler, *The Act of Creation,* p. 514.

6. *Ibid.* This concept of alternative and potentially exclusive modes of perception is closely related to the theory of a "perceptual set." As defined by Cherry, *op. cit.,* pp. 275–77, "A person's psychological 'set' toward some task, situation, or communication event depends upon a host of preceding events which have led up to that moment. Such a 'set' is considered to influence his formation of associations, by bringing to bear certain 'determining tendencies,' and hence influencing his way of organizing or executing the task, or affecting the degree to which he recognizes signs, or forms perceptions, in a communication event." The importance of this formation of a psychological "set" toward communication events is best grasped if it is understood that information transfer is a matter of selection of alternatives. "Information can be received only where there is doubt; and doubt implies the existence of alternatives—where choice, selection, or discrimination is called for. . . . Now it is customary to speak of signals as 'conveying information,' as though information were a kind of commodity. But signals do not convey information as railway trucks carry coal. Rather we should say: signals have an information content by virtue of the *potential for making selections.* Signals operate upon the alternatives forming the recipient's

doubt . . . they give the power to discriminate amongst, or select from, these alternatives" (p. 170). Thus, rather than transfer information, signals seem to allow information in an unborn state to come to the surface of the human consciousness. What impulse goes into the organism is certainly not more important than what discriminating matrices the impulse must go through. A correlative would be that what impulse comes out of the organism—the behavior and the modes of communication chosen by the individual —are a reflection of the nature of the discriminating mechanisms. The product speaks of the process. Since much of this process is subconscious, perhaps preconscious activity, it can be suggested that the very communication modes chosen by a culture are part of an internal drive for cultural exclusivity, perhaps as an extension of the individual's personality through group activity, and hence the potential amplification of that personality.

7. Stokely Carmichael, "The Black Princes," London *Sunday Times* magazine, November 2, 1969, p. 28.

8. Huey Newton, "Essays from the Minister of Defense."

9. On October 4, 1969, *Rolling Stone* magazine reported "Elaine Brown, Deputy Minister of Information of the Black Panther Party . . . signed a contract with Vault Records; her first LP, consisting of political songs written by Miss Brown . . . is a political act, Miss Brown says, designed to give the Panther Party a new avenue of communication to people." One wonders why an organization which is, according to its own publicity, a prime voice for the black ghetto, failed to grasp the essentially revolutionary medium of records sooner, and further why, in fact, their use of the medium was so poorly handled. The LP, blatantly dogmatic, indicates a failure to understand that black music in America, by its very nature, is revolutionary and this quality is only submerged by highly sophisticated and rationalized lyrics.

10. Quoted in *Jazz*, Nat Hentoff & Albert McCarthy, p. 23.

11. See J.F. Carrington, *The Talking Drums of Africa* or *The Drum Language of the Lokele Tribe.*

12. Quoted in M.J. Herskovitz, *The Myth of the Negro Past,* p. 291.

13. McLuhan, *op. cit.*, p. 59.

14. There is great public interest in the concept of "noise pollution," for example, and some researchers claim to have isolated a way of measuring the "effective perceptive noise level," which gauges human response to noise rather than decibel level. Several groups are also working on the influence of amplified music on the individual musician (notably the team of Dr. Ray Reddell at the San Francisco Hearing Center). On an even more general level, Dr. P. Weinberger, a biology researcher at the University of Ottawa informed me that she has found corn, cucumbers, peas, and oats grow "quite definitely taller, stronger, and leafier when recorded folk songs were played to them." She insisted that the increased growth of those subjected to music was between 15 and 20 percent more than those left in silence. (For more results of Dr. Weinberger's work, see *Canadian Journal of Botany,* Vol. 46, September 1968, pp. 1151–61.)

15. Raymond Williams, *op. cit.*, p. 40.

16. Desmond Morris, in *The Naked Ape,* p. 90, cites an experiment that suggests that the mother's heartbeat has these effects and that "a metronome imitation" of the natural rhythm of a heartbeat would not produce the same results. Morris has also linked rhythmic activity with the release from boredom in various articles—see *Sun Times Weekly Review,* November 2, 1969, p. 49.

17. Rainer Werning, "Tribe Time," *International Times,* May 31, 1968.

18. "Structure of feeling," a concept developed by Raymond Williams, represents that "most difficult thing to get hold of, in studying any past period . . . [that] felt sense of the quality of life at a particular place and time: a sense of the ways in which the particular activities combined into a way of thinking and living," *op. cit.*, p. 63.

19. McLuhan, *op. cit.*, p. 135.

20. Wilfred Mellers, *Music in a New Found Land,* p. 291.

21. Raymond Williams, *op. cit.*, p. 55.

22. Alfred Hayes, "Black English: Extension of a Way of Life," *International Herald Tribune,* November 6, 1969.

23. Quoted in Herskovitz, *op. cit.*, p. 280.

24. See Ludwig Wittgenstein, *Philosophical Investigations.*

25. Milton Metfessel, *Phonophotography in Folk Music.* This interpretation is a significant departure from the traditional Western approach to the diatonic scale, as characterized in an early text by Percy Goetchius, *The Theory and Practice of Tone-Relations.* New York: Schirmer Inc., 1931, p. 3: "From the infinite multitude of possible tones perceptible to the ear," writes Goetchius, "the intuition of man (in civilized countries) has singled out a limited number (at first 7, later 12), which, with their reproduction or duplication in higher and lower registers, by the octave relation, represent the entire absolute tone-material of the art of music." Black music, apparently, originates from an "uncivilized" source, and hence, is not to be bound by these rules.

26. Cherry, *op. cit.*, p. 45.

27. See, recently, Frank George, "Simulating Human Thought," *Science Journal,* January 1970, pp. 56–60.

28. John Coltrane, *Jazz & Pop,* September 1967, p. 26.

29. W.E.B. Du Bois, *The Souls of Black Folk,* p. 17.

30. William Grier & Price Cobbs, *Black Rage,* p. 150.

31. LeRoi Jones, *Blues People,* p. 80.

32. See Mellers, *op. cit.*, p. 262: "In discussing the genesis of American popular music in the late nineteenth century we observed that both its positive and negative poles, as represented by Sousa and Foster respectively, were an evasion of 'reality,' whether through oversimplification or through escape. Jazz, which was ultimately to affect popular music all over the world, flowed parallel to the streams of Foster and Sousa, yet differed from them in that it flowed on the hardest rockbed of reality. It began as the music of a minority, a dispossessed race. This minority, having nothing more to lose, could accept alienation and its isolation to the members of an ostensibly prosperous society."

33. Herskovitz, *op. cit.*, p. 217.

34. Charles Parker, quoted in *The Legend of Charlie Parker,* Robert Reisner, p. 27.

35. Ornette Coleman, quoted in A. B. Spellman, *Four Lives in the Bebop Business*, pp. 142–43.

36. See Stanley Elkins, *Slavery*, 1963.

37. *Ibid.*, p. 40.

38. A. Bavelas, "Communication Patterns in Task Oriented Groups," *Journal of Acoustic Society of America,* November 22, 1950, p. 725.

39. McLuhan, *op. cit.*, p. 246.

40. Jones, *op. cit.*, p. 66.

41. Hobbes took the abstraction of the "bare human being" for granted and rarely considered relationships of any sort. Locke introduced the element of society as an arrangement to ensure the abstract rights of the individual (bare human being). Rousseau, likewise, considered relationships as part of a larger "social contract." Hegel introduced the notion of the community as mediating element between the individual and the society at large and added the more fluent concept of "class" which is different from the more static "order." Marx exploited this notion to its fullest. This tradition of Western Individualism clearly develops the idea that man is basically separate from his society and from his environment and that he needs protection through the mediation of categories. Oral cultures do not begin from the assumption of the separation of man from man, nor of man from environment, and thus the tradition of Western Individualism—which was ultimately used to justify the institution of slavery—is not useful for the analysis of oral activities and individuals.

42. Norman Mailer, "Looking for the Meat and Potatoes—Thoughts on Black Power," *Look,* January 7, 1969, p. 58.

43. *Ibid.*, p. 59.

44. Quoted in Martin Williams, *Jazz Panorama,* p. 73.

2. THE BLACK MUSICIAN IN TWO AMERICAS

1. Eldridge Cleaver, *Post-Prison Writing and Speeches*, p. 129.

2. Address delivered before the Georgia House of Representa-

tives, September 3, 1868, by Henry Turner, quoted in *Chronicles of Black Protest*, Bradford Chambers, ed., p. 131.

3. From text of Booker T. Washington's "Atlanta Compromise" speech, *ibid.*, p. 144.

4. Milton Gordon, *Assimilation in American Life*, p. 88.

5. Quoted in Silberman, *Crisis in Black and White*, p. 142.

6. Frantz Fanon, *Black Skin, White Masks*, p. 98.

7. Wilder Hobson, *American Jazz Music*, p. 36.

8. Folkways Records, Leadbelly Anthology, Vol. II.

9. Harold Isaacs, *The New World of Negro Americans*, p. 339.

10. J.W. Work, *American Negro Songs & Spirituals*, pp. 34–35.

11. Grier & Cobbs, *op. cit.*, p. 50.

12. Charles Keil, *Urban Blues*, p. 20.

13. One of the extreme examples of this extraordinary situation, but not an uncommon one, was the plight of the tobacco workers of Manchester, Va. Before emancipation, the black workers received room, board, and lodging for doing work their masters got paid for. In addition, they were given $9 to $10 per week for the work they did in excess of the task set. After emancipation, wages dropped to a point where blacks could not earn more than $5 per week, and they no longer received food and lodging!

14. Bunk Johnson quoted in *Hear Me Talkin' to Ya*, Nat Hentoff and Nat Shapiro, p. 36.

15. Quoted in Marshall Stearns, *The Story of Jazz*, p. 57.

16. Clarence Williams, quoted in *Hear Me Talkin' to Ya*, Hentoff & Shapiro, p. 32.

17. George Baguet, *ibid.*, p. 38.

18. Louis Armstrong, *ibid.*, p. 39.

19. Danny Barker, *ibid.*, p. 26.

20. *Ibid.*, p. 1.

21. Babs Gonzales, *I Paid My Dues*, pp. 17–18.

22. Danny Barker, quoted in *Hear Me Talkin' to Ya*, Hentoff & Shapiro, p. 52.

23. Desmond Morris, *The Human Zoo,* p. 38.

24. Wingy Manone quoted in *Hear Me Talkin' to Ya,* Hentoff & Shapiro, p. 25.

25. From *Jazzmen,* Ramsey & Smith, p. 12.

26. Paul Domingue quoted in Alan Lomax, *Mr. Jelly Roll,* pp. 15–16.

27. *Vodun* was a religious cult derived from the Dahomean tribes brought to America during slavery. Its central characteristics were a belief in possession by spirits and, subsequently, ancestor worship. While slaves ostensibly practiced Christianity, often the Christian services shrouded vestigial *vodun* ritual. Often the *vodun* ritual was carried on knowingly, in secret. This form of spiritualism, with all its magical trappings, survives today in the Negro communities of America. In its nineteenth-century form, the *vodun* cults drew large numbers from the poorer, more rural Negroes, thus the basis for its becoming a substantial part of the secret society system when the secularization process of the twentieth century took hold. Today, the charms and magic fetishes, such as "John the Conquering Root" and the "Mojo" are found in Northern cities as well as in the South, and one urban musician told me, "Voodoo, that shit ain't nothing . . . but watch out!"

28. Herskovitz, *op. cit.,* p. 215.

29. Quoted in Mellers, *op. cit.,* p. 302.

30. Herskovitz, *op. cit.,* p. 164.

31. Quoted in *Gumbo Ya-Ya,* Saxon, Dreyer & Tallant, pp. 311–12.

32. Bunk Johnson, liner notes, *New Orleans Parade,* American Music Records, 101–03.

33. Quoted in *Hear Me Talkin' to Ya,* Hentoff & Shapiro, p. 249.

34. Quoted in Martin Williams, *Jazz Panorama, op. cit.,* p. 77.

35. Norman Margolis, "A Theory on the Psychology of Jazz," *The American Image,* Vol. II, No. 3, Fall, 1954, pp. 372–73.

36. Jones, *Blues People, op. cit.,* pp. 153–54.

3. THE JAZZ AGE

1. J.A. Rogers, "Jazz at Home," *Survey*, March 1, 1925, p. 665.

2. Marcus Garvey, speech titled, "The Principles of the Universal Negro, Improvement Association," delivered at Liberty Hall, New York, November 25, 1922.

3. *Ibid.*

4. Grier & Cobbs, *op. cit.*, p. 105.

5. Mutt Carey, quoted in *Hear Me Talkin' to Ya*, Hentoff & Shapiro, p. 46.

6. Louis Armstrong, *Swing That Music*, pp. 52–53.

7. For the most perceptive analysis, see *Radical Software*, published by Raindance Corp., 24 E. 22nd St., New York City, N.Y.

8. In actual fact, phonograph records created whole styles of blues playing as well as altering the form of blues playing. See especially, "Recording Limits and Blues Form" in *The Art of Jazz*, Martin Williams, pp. 91–92.

9. Cecil Taylor quoted in Spellman, *op. cit.*, p. 31.

10. Quoted in Stearns, *op. cit.*, p. 73.

11. Paul Whiteman & Mary Margaret McBride, *Jazz*, p. 94.

12. Eldridge Cleaver, *Soul on Ice*, p. 79.

13. Quoted in Silberman, *Crisis in Black and White*, p. 52.

14. Quoted in *Hear Me Talkin' to Ya*, Hentoff & Shapiro, p. 111.

15. Martin Oppenheimer, *Urban Guerrilla*, p. 22.

16. André Hodeir, *Jazz: Its Evolution and Essence*, p. 51.

17. Mellers, *op. cit.*, p. 301.

18. Quoted in Williams, *Jazz Panorama*, *op. cit.*, p. 101.

19. Quoted in Hentoff & Shapiro, *op. cit.*, p. 313.

4. THE EVOLUTION OF THE BLACK
   UNDERGROUND

1. See, for example, *Jazz Era*, Stanley Dance, ed., p. 22.

2. Francis Newton, *The Jazz Scene*, p. 257. (Francis Newton is Eric Hobsbaum.)

3. Robert Ardrey, *The Territorial Imperative*, p. 272.

4. The T.O.B.A. circuit was known among black musicians as the "tough on black artists" circuit. This is perhaps the earliest time the phrase *black artists* was used by Negro musicians to describe themselves.

5. Idea suggested by Rupert Wilkinson, English & American Studies, University of Sussex.

6. Quoted in Newton, *op. cit.*, p. 216.

7. Miles Davis quoted in *Rolling Stone*, December 27, 1969, p. 17.

8. Jones, *Blues People, op. cit.*, p. 172.

9. Quoted in Charles Keil, *op. cit.*, p. 64.

10. Hsio Wen Shih, "The Spread of Jazz and the Big Bands," in *Jazz*, Hentoff & McCarthy, p. 72.

11. Quoted in Hentoff & Shapiro, *op. cit.*, p. 329.

12. *Ibid.*, p. 284.

13. Benny Goodman and Irving Kolodin, *The Kingdom of Swing*, p. 241.

14. Quoted in Stanley Dance, *op. cit.*, p. 40.

15. Ian Lang, *Jazz in Perspective*, p. 99.

16. See Billie Holiday, *Lady Sings the Blues*.

17. See Ross Russell, "The Parent Style and Lester Young," *The Art of Jazz*, Martin Williams, p. 210.

18. Stearns, *op. cit.*, p. 215.

19. Newton, *op. cit.*, p. 267.

20. Isaacs, *op. cit.*, p. 42.

21. Quoted in Benjamin Quarles, *The Negro in the Making of America*, p. 216.

22. *Ibid.*, p. 223.

23. Hentoff & Shapiro, *op. cit.*, p. 354.

24. Quoted in Ira Gitler, *Jazz Masters of the Forties*, p. 34.

25. Quoted in Reisner, *op. cit.*, p. 194.

26. Miles Davis quoted in *Down Beat* magazine, November 2, 1955, p. 14.

27. Ross Russell, "Bebop," *The Art of Jazz*, Martin Williams, p. 189.

28. Jones, *Blues People, op. cit.*, p. 194.

29. Stearns, *op. cit.*, p. 157.

30. Reisner, *op. cit.*, p. 230.

31. *Ibid.*, p. 13.

32. Morris, *The Human Zoo*, p. 29.

33. See Milton Mezzrow and Bernard Wolfe, *Really the Blues*.

34. Grier & Cobbs, *op. cit.*, p. 56.

35. It is interesting to note, however, that it was not heroin which caused Parker's collapse but rather an overdose of methedrine administered by a well-meaning doctor who didn't realize that Parker had been staying awake on stimulants for several days. Mistaking the symptoms for heroin withdrawal, he administered the stimulant, and several hours later Parker suffered a "nervous collapse."

36. Quoted in Reisner, *op. cit.*, p. 52.

37. *Ibid.*

38. See Howard Becker, *Outsiders*, chapters 1, 5, and 6.

5. BLACK VISIBILITY

1. From the text of the National Advisory Commission on Civil Disorders report, microfilm, University of Wisconsin Library.

2. From the text of the *Newsweek* national survey as reported in "The Forgotten Majority," October 6, 1969, pp. 20–31.

3. From the text of the National Council of Churches statement, *The New York Times,* July 31, 1966.

4. Claude Brown, *Manchild in the Promised Land,* p. 101.

5. Howard Brotz, *The Black Jews of Harlem,* p. 5.

6. Brown, *op. cit.,* p. 101.

7. *Ibid.,* p. 165.

8. Quoted in Joe Goldberg, *Jazz Masters of the Fifties,* p. 77.

9. Quoted in Hentoff & Shapiro, *op. cit.,* p. 397.

10. Quoted in *Black Power Revolt,* Floyd Barbour, p. 215.

11. Edward Harvey, "Social Change and the Jazz Musician," *Social Forces,* September 1967.

12. Quoted in Isaacs, *op. cit.,* p. 52.

13. Brown, *op. cit.,* p. 166.

14. Quoted in Spellman, *op. cit.,* p. 145.

15. See Theodore Roszak, *The Making of a Counter-Culture.*

16. Nat Hentoff, "The Life Perspectives of the New Jazz," *Down Beat Yearbook,* 1967, p. 22.

17. Abbie Hoffman, *Woodstock Nation,* p. 26.

18. Abbie Hoffman, *Revolution for the Hell of It,* p. 9.

19. Quoted in Eldridge Cleaver, *Post-Prison Writing and Speeches,* p. 50. Also see Carmichael's developing approach to actional ideology published as *Aframerican Report,* available from Student Voice, Inc., 360 Nelson St., S. Atlanta, Georgia.

20. Quoted in Spellman, *op. cit.,* p. 62.

21. Stokely Carmichael, "What We Want," *New York Review of Books,* September 22, 1966.

22. Cleaver, *Soul on Ice,* p. 3.

23. Quoted in Silberman, *op. cit.,* p. 156.

24. Quoted in Spellman, *op. cit.,* p. 234.

25. Coleman liner notes, *Change of the Century*, Atlantic records, 1327.

26. Quoted in Spellman, *op. cit.*, p. 119.

27. *Ibid.*, p. 120.

28. Quoted in Goldberg, *op. cit.*, p. 204.

29. *Ibid.*, p. 199.

30. Quoted in "John Coltrane," *Jazz & Pop*, September 1967, p. 26.

31. Malcolm X, "The Ballot or the Bullet" speech, New York City, March 22, 1964.

32. Robert Williams, *Negroes With Guns*, "Self Defense and American Tradition."

33. Quoted in Spellman, *op. cit.*, p. 8.

34. Cecil Taylor, "Point of Contact," *Down Beat Yearbook*, 1966, pp. 19–31.

35. This survey, done at Discount Records Inc. stores by Ben Sidran and Morgan Usadel, had many and various aspects. For example, it noted the difference in record purchasing habits of fraternity members as opposed to those of "independents." The results were used both to plan the physical layout of the shops, i.e., what record bin should be closest to the front to get maximum coverage and to determine store policy, i.e., which students should be hired in light of what kind of musical knowledge was required to fill the needs of the customers. The findings confirmed that black music was the mainstay of the political "radical" whites whereas white popular music was more generally accepted by a broad base of white students. Significantly, when student demonstrations disrupted all three of these campuses, the local Discount Record store was left undamaged, although other record stores were vandalized. In Berkeley, the record shop became the temporary headquarters for radical students during the occupation by the National Guard.

36. Jeff Nuttall, *Bomb Culture*, p. 20.

37. Quoted in *Jazz & Pop*, *op. cit.*, p. 28.

38. Malcolm X, "Letter from Mecca" dated Jedda, Saudi Arabia, April 20, 1964.

39. See especially "Rules of the Black Panther Party." *The Black Panther,* September 13, 1969.

40. Quoted in *Down Beat Yearbook,* 1966, *op. cit.,* pp. 19–31.

41. Stewart Alsop, "Nixon and the Anti-Kid Vote," *Newsweek,* June 15, 1970, p. 23.

42. Silberman, *op. cit.,* p. 15.

43. Du Bois, *op. cit.,* p. 117.

44. A. Cecil Williams quoted in Liberation News Service bulletin, week of June 8, 1970.

45. Herbert Hendin, "Young Negro Suicide Rate," *Capitol Times,* July 31, 1969, p. 19.

46. Charles Hamilton & Stokely Carmichael, *Black Power: The Politics of Liberation in America,* p. 183.

SELECTED BIBLIOGRAPHY

Aframerican Report, Vol. I, Nos. 1–3. Student Voice Inc. Atlanta, Georgia.

Ardrey, Robert, *The Territorial Imperative*. New York: Dell, 1966.

Armstrong, Louis, *Swing That Music*. New York: Longmans, Green, 1936.

Barbour, Floyd, ed., *Black Power Revolt*. Toronto: Macmillan, 1968.

Bavelas, A., "Communication Patterns in Task Oriented Groups," *Journal of Acoustic Society of America*. November 22, 1950.

Becker, Howard, *Outsiders*. New York: Free Press, 1963.

Brotz, Howard, *The Black Jews of Harlem*. New York: Free Press, 1964.

Brown, Claude, *Manchild in the Promised Land*. New York: Macmillan, 1966.

Carmichael, Stokely, "The Black Princes," London *Sunday Times* magazine, November 2, 1969.
"What We Want," *New York Review of Books*, September 22, 1966.

Carrington, J.F., *The Drum Language of the Lokele Tribe*. Witwatersrand: Witwatersrand University Press, 1944.
The Talking Drums of Africa. London: Carey Kingsgate Press, 1949.

Chambers, Bradford, ed., *Chronicles of Black Protest*. New York: Mentor, 1968.

Cherry, Colin, *On Human Communication*. Cambridge, Mass.: M.I.T. Press, 1968.

Cleaver, Eldridge, *Post-Prison Writing and Speeches*. New York: Random House, 1969.
Soul on Ice. New York: Dell, 1968.

177

Coleman, Ornette, liner notes, *Change of the Century*, Atlantic Records, 1327.

Dance, Stanley, *Jazz Era*, London: Macgibbon & Kee, 1961.

Du Bois, W.E.B., *The Souls of Black Folk*. New York: Fawcett, 1961.

Elkins, Stanley, *Slavery*. New York: Grosset, 1963.

Fanon, Frantz, *Black Skin, White Masks*. New York: Grove Press, 1967.
    The Wretched of the Earth. Middlesex: Penguin, 1967.

Feather, Leonard, *The Book of Jazz*. New York: Horizon, 1957.
    Inside Bebop. New York: J.J. Robbins, 1949.

Finkelstein, Sidney, *Jazz: A People's Music*. New York: Citadel, 1948.

George, Frank, "Simulating Human Thought," *Science Journal*, January 1970.

Gitler, Ira, *Jazz Masters of the Forties*. New York: Macmillan, 1966.

Gleason, Ralph, *Jam Session*. New York: G.P. Putnam, 1958.

Goetchius, Percy, *The Theory and Practice of Tone-Relations*. New York: Schirmer, 1931.

Goldberg, Joe, *Jazz Masters of the Fifties*. New York: Macmillan, 1965.

Gonzales, Babs, *I Paid My Dues*. East Orange, N.J.: Expubidence Publishing Corp., 1967.

Goodman, Benny & Irving Kolodin, *The Kingdom of Swing*. Harrisburg: Stackpole & Sons, 1939.

Gordon, Milton, *Assimilation in American Life*. Oxford: Oxford University Press, 1964.

Grier, William & Price Cobbs, *Black Rage*. New York: Bantam, 1968.

Hamilton, Charles & Stokely Carmichael, *Black Power: The Politics of Liberation in America*. Middlesex: Penguin, 1969.

Harrison, Max, *Charlie Parker*. New York: A.S. Barnes, 1961.

Harvey, Edward, "Social Change and the Jazz Musician," *Social Forces*, September 1967.

Hayes, Alfred, "Black English: Extension of a Way of Life," *International Herald Tribune*, November 6, 1969.

Hentoff, Nat, "The Life Perspectives of the New Jazz," *Down Beat Yearbook*, 1967.

Hentoff, Nat & Albert McCarthy, eds., *Jazz*. New York: Rinehart, 1959.

Hentoff, Nat & Nat Shapiro, *The Jazz Makers*. New York: Rinehart, 1957.

Hentoff, Nat & Nat Shapiro, *Hear Me Talkin' to Ya*. New York: Dover, 1955.

Herskovitz, M.J., *The Myth of the Negro Past*. Boston: Beacon Press, 1958.

Hobson, Wilder, *American Jazz Music*. New York: Norton, 1939.

Hodeir, André, *Jazz: Evolution and Essence*. New York: Grove Press, 1961.

Hoffman, Abbie, *Revolution for the Hell of It*. New York: Dial Press, 1968.
Woodstock Nation. New York: Random House, 1969.

Holiday, Billie, *Lady Sings the Blues*. New York: Lancer, 1965.

Huxley, Aldous, *The Doors of Perception*. New York: Harper, 1954.

Isaacs, Harold, *The New World of Negro Americans*. London: J.M. Dent & Sons, 1963.

Jones, LeRoi, *Black Music*. London: Macgibbon & Kee, 1969.
Blues People. New York: Morrow, 1963.

Keepnews, Orrin & Bill Grauer, Jr., *A Pictorial History of Jazz*. New York: Crown, 1966.

Keil, Charles, *Urban Blues*. Chicago: University of Chicago Press, 1966.

Koestler, Arthur, *The Act of Creation*. London: Hutchinson, 1964.

Lambert, G.E., *Duke Ellington*. New York: A.S. Barnes, 1961.

Lang, Ian, *Jazz in Perspective*. London: Hutchinson, 1957.

Lester, Julius, *Look Out, Whitey! Black Power's Gon' Get Your Mama!* New York: Grove Press, 1968.

Lévi-Strauss, Claude, *The Savage Mind*. London: Weidenfeld & Nicolson, 1966.

Lomax, Alan, *Mister Jelly Roll*. New York: Evergreen, 1968.

Lorenz, Konrad, *On Aggression*. New York: Harcourt, 1966.

Mailer, Norman, "Looking for the Meat and Potatoes—Thoughts on Black Power," *Look,* January 7, 1969.

Malcolm X, *The Autobiography of Malcolm X*. New York: Grove Press, 1962.

Margolis, Norman, "A Theory on the Psychology of Jazz," *The American Image,* Vol. II, No. 3, Fall, 1954.

McLuhan, Marshall, *Understanding Media*. New York: Signet, 1964.

McRae, Barry, *Jazz Cataclysm*. New York: A.S. Barnes, 1967.

Mellers, Wilfred, *Music in a New Found Land*. London: Barrie & Rockliff, 1964.

Metfessel, Milton, *Phonophotography in Folk Music*. Chapel Hill: University of North Carolina Press, 1928.

Mezzrow, Milton & Bernard Wolfe, *Really the Blues*. New York: Random House, 1946.

Morris, Desmond, *The Human Zoo*. London: Jonathan Cape Ltd., 1969.
The Naked Ape. New York: Dell, 1969.

Newton, Francis, *The Jazz Scene*. London: Macgibbon & Kee, 1960.

Newton, Huey, "Essays From the Minister of Defense." (No publishing information given.)

Nuttall, Jeff, *Bomb Culture*. London: Paladin, 1970.

Oppenheimer, Martin, *Urban Guerrilla*. Middlesex: Penguin, 1969.

Quarles, Benjamin, *The Negro in the Making of America*. London: Collier, 1969.

Ramsey, Frederic & Charles Edward Smith, *Jazzmen*. New York: Harcourt, 1939.

Reisner, Robert, *The Legend of Charlie Parker*. New York: Bonanza, 1962.

Rogers, J.A., "Jazz at Home," *Survey*, March 1, 1925.

Roszak, Theodore, *The Making of a Counter-Culture*. New York: Doubleday, 1969.

Saxon, Dreyer & Tallant, eds., *Gumbo Ya-Ya*. Boston: Houghton Mifflin, 1945.

Silberman, Charles, *Crisis in Black and White*. New York: Random House, 1964.

Spellman, A.B., *Four Lives in the Bebop Business*. New York: Pantheon, 1966.

Stearns, Marshall, *The Story of Jazz*. New York: Mentor, 1958. (The most comprehensive bibliography on jazz and the jazz business, compiled by Robert Reisner, is included at the back of this edition.)

Ulanov, Barry, *A Handbook of Jazz*. New York: Viking, 1957. *A History of Jazz in America*. New York: Viking, 1952.

Weinberger, Pearl, "The effect of two audible sound frequencies on the germination and growth of a spring and winter wheat," *Canadian Journal of Botany*, September 1968.

Werning, Rainer, "Tribe Time," *International Times*, May 31, 1968.

Whiteman, Paul & Mary Margaret McBride, *Jazz*. New York: J.H. Sears, 1926.

Williams, Martin, *The Art of Jazz*. New York: Oxford Press, 1959.
Jazz Panorama. New York: Harcourt, 1939.

Williams, Raymond, *The Long Revolution*. London: Cox & Wyman Ltd., 1961.

Williams, Robert, *Negroes With Guns*. New York: Marzani & Munsell, 1962.

Wittgenstein, Ludwig, *Philosophical Investigations*. New York: Macmillan, 1966.

Work, J.W., *American Negro Songs & Spirituals*. New York: Crown, 1940.

A valuable source of information have been the liner notes from many Blue Note, Impulse, Prestige, and Riverside records. A complete list of all available American jazz records is found in the monthly *Schwann* catalogue, 137 Newbury Street, Boston, Mass. I have also used *Down Beat, Jazz & Pop, Rolling Stone, Jazz Journal,* and *Jazz Monthly* magazines for general source material.

CHRONOLOGY

1619   Twenty Negroes brought to Jamestown, Virginia, as bondsmen to English settlers.

1830   Federal census shows over 3,000 Negro families own slaves.

1830   (approx.) Minstrelsy becomes popular in white society, continues to present day, particularly in England.

1831   Nat Turner leads slave revolt.

1860   (approx.) Black minstrel tradition develops in the South, continues well into the twentieth century as training ground for black musicians (i.e., Ornette Coleman worked with a minstrel band as late as 1947).

1863   Emancipation Proclamation marks theoretical beginning of secular music tradition; "devil music" becomes early blues; and the black musician begins to take on social functions of black preacher.

1867   Reconstruction Act passed by Congress gives Negroes the vote.

1876   Reconstruction ends. President Hayes withdraws troops from the South. Failure of Reconstruction one source of "worldly cynicism" in blues idiom.

1885   Congo Square in New Orleans closed down; *vodun* rituals become important as non-Christian source of spirituality and rhythmic reservoir.

1895   Booker T. Washington's "Atlanta Compromise" speech propounds the "separate-but-equal" philosophy.

1896   "Black Codes" and "peonage laws" appear throughout the South, socially and economically segregating Negroes and whites. *Plessy v. Ferguson* case finds Supreme Court upholding the "separate-but-equal" doctrine. Creole musicians in New Orleans forced back into lower-class musical tradition. Buddy Bolden forms first "jazz" band, combining marching band instrumentation with blues technique.

1898–1917   New Orleans community flourishes. Jazz musicians grow from casual musicians into professionals.

1906   "Niagara Movement" led by W.E.B. Du Bois.

1917   America's entry into World War I forces Storyville district of New Orleans to close down. Original Dixieland Jazz Band, white musicians from New Orleans, score great success in New York.

1919   Chicago race riots mark the Negro's entry into the social process of Northern urban communities.

1920   Mamie Smith records "Crazy Blues," first recorded "hit" by black artist; marks the beginning of "race records."

1923   Marcus Garvey's UNIA claims a membership of over half a million Negroes.

1924   Paul Whiteman's Aeolian Hall concert brings "jazz" to the elite of white society.

1926   Louis Armstrong records "Hot Five" numbers with a Chicago pick-up band.

1927   Duke Ellington opens at the Cotton Club in New York.

1929   Stock market collapse ends affluence and assimilative trends of the "Jazz Age" and plunges black Americans into cultural isolation.

1930   W.D. Fard starts Black Muslim movement.

1932   Kansas City blues resurgence; rhythm-and-blues becomes a recognizable urban idiom.

1934   Count Basie takes over Bennie Moten's band.

1935   Benny Goodman hailed as the "King of Swing."

1939   Charles Parker makes his harmonic breakthrough while rehearsing the changes to "Cherokee" in a New York City chile house.

1941   Pearl Harbor; World War II brings with it a confrontation between Nazi racism and totalitarianism and American democracy. One result was to highlight lack of democracy and racism within American society.

1945   Charlie Parker and Dizzy Gillespie lead a group on 52nd Street. Hip ethic and drug-use become noticeable among bop musicians.

1947   52nd Street closed down.

1949   Miles Davis/Gil Evans, *Birth of the Cool* recording, the origin of the "cool" school of jazz playing and a reflection of the "wait-and-see" attitude of blacks following the war.

1954   *Brown v. Board of Education* decision nullifies the "separate-but-equal" precedent established in 1896.

1955   Jazz Messengers formed; "The Preacher" one of the first "soul" hits; initial stages of the "soul" movement and a new sense of community in black culture become evident. Cultural self-definition and drug-use cross paths.

1956   Robert Williams's *Negroes With Guns.*

1958   Miles Davis's *Kind of Blue.*

1960   SNCC formed in the South. White youth join black culture in new social "cause."

1961   John Coltrane's quartet with Elvin Jones shows new "spiritual" intensity.

1964   *Student as Nigger* pamphlet circulated on college campuses.

1965   Malcolm X shot, allegedly by Black Muslims. Riots in Watts the worst of the modern era.

1967   John Coltrane dies; Pharoah Sanders and "energy" players emerge. Summer known as "the long hot summer" because of civil disorder. President Johnson appoints Otto Kerner to chair an inquiry into racial disturbances. "Riot commission" reports that racist attitude of whites causes black disaffection and is leading America toward "two separate societies, one white, one black, separate but unequal." The report, issued in 1968, is ignored by the President and the population in general.

1968/1969   Twenty-nine Black Panthers killed by police throughout the United States.

1969   Pharoah Sanders records with B.B. King at a live concert at the Fillmore East.

INDEX